UNTO THE UTTERMOST

The Richard Walkers and the Amazon Mission Organization

Claude Sumerlin

VANTAGE PRESS
New York

To my wife, Katherine

FIRST EDITION

All rights reserved, including the right of
reproduction in whole or in part in any form.

Copyright © 1996 by Claude Sumerlin

Published by Vantage Press, Inc.
516 West 34th Street, New York, New York 10001

Manufactured in the United States of America
ISBN: 0-533-11624-4

Library of Congress Catalog Card No.: 95-94755

0 9 8 7 6 5 4 3 2 1

Foreword

The first time I met Richard Walker, he presented himself as a quiet, humble, unassuming missionary. As he handed me a modest brochure about AMOR, the Amazon River Mission Organization, he simply said, "Read this over and if you're interested, I'll be glad to give you more information about our ministry." Little did I know that the man before me was truly the apostle of the Amazon. I was later to learn that Richard and Bea Walker and their sons, Boyd and Winston, had literally taken the gospel throughout the vast Amazon Basin. I would soon know that this family had brought the glorious light of the gospel of Jesus Christ into the dark regions of the Amazon in a powerful and dynamic way.

Richard and Bea Walker are unique. The power of God upon their lives is evidenced in their godly humility and powerful ministry. I have been privileged to be on the Amazon with the Walkers and to have seen firsthand the impact of their work. I have seen the quiet, unassuming missionary transformed into a dynamo of compassion, vision, discernment, and a powerful proclaimer of the gospel. I have seen Richard Walker take the weak, the sick, the feeble, the little child into his arms and offer words of encouragement and enlightenment in the beautiful Portuguese language. I've seen the respect that the Brazilians have for this man and his family. I can truly say that one of the greatest honors of my life is to be asked to write the foreword for this book, which details the Walkers' lives and ministry in the jungles of the Amazon.

I encourage every reader to ask yourself the question, "Lord, what would you have me do to help the Walkers take the gospel into the dark, hopeless jungles of the Amazon?" There are many peoples on the tributaries and lakes of this mighty river who have never even heard the name of Jesus. You can be a part of one of the most powerful missionary endeavors of our generation by praying for and participating with AMOR to take the gospel to these receptive people. The

Amazon is unbelievable in size. Pushing fresh water 120 miles out to the Atlantic Ocean, it takes the flow of the next five largest rivers in the world to equal the flow of the Amazon. The Amazon Basin is a massive area with an open door for the gospel. The mammoth size of the river is paralleled with the mammoth-sized opportunity to present the gospel of Jesus Christ to these beautiful people.

Thank you, Richard, Bea, Boyd, and Winston for allowing me the great privilege of helping in a small way with your ministry and thank you for reflecting the powerful love of Jesus Christ in such a dynamic way. The Portuguese word for love is *amor*. Richard Walker defines love as "the unsolicited giving of the best you have on behalf of another regardless of response." Dr. Walker, you have defined your life and ministry.

—Sam Bailey
Pastor of Twin Lakes Baptist Church
Mountain Home, Arkansas

Chapter 1

When Richard and Bea Walker sailed from New Orleans with their two young sons on August 19, 1964, as Southern Baptist missionaries to Brazil, little did they realize how deeply their entire family and perhaps future grandchildren would be involved in meeting both the spiritual and physical needs of remote villagers along the mighty Amazon and its tributaries. But the young couple was sure of God's calling and was willing to go wherever He led. They would, however, find their pathway to missionary service strewn with many obstacles.

Both were born to middle-class working families. Richard was born March 10, 1932, the seventh of twelve children to Otis and Mary Ellon Walker in Texas City, Texas, where his father owned a wholesale-retail gasoline business. The middle child grew up among eight brothers and three sisters. After the birth of the last child, Richard's father decided it would be best to move the family away from the fast-growing Texas coastal town.

When Richard was twelve years of age, his family moved from Texas City and arrived at their new home in Berryville, Carroll County, in northwest Arkansas, on Halloween Eve, 1944. He recalls that instead of firecrackers, exploding sticks of dynamite, used to celebrate the holiday festivities, greeted their arrival.

Beatrice (or Bea as she became known), on the other hand, was born on July 29, 1933, to W. C. and Mollie Rodgers on a farm in the Sardis community near the little mining town of Bauxite, Arkansas. Her father was a heavy equipment operator for fifty years with the Aluminum Company of America, while her mother worked as a nurse's aide in Benton. Their older son died later in life of cancer.

While still in high school, Bea felt the call to missions while participating in a musical program at Pleasant Hill Baptist Church in the Sardis community. When she confided this to her parents, her mother commented, "If you only had a husband . . ."

The future missionary was graduated from Bauxite High School in 1951 and received her registered nurse degree from St. Vincent's Infirmary in Little Rock in 1954. During her senior year in nursing school, she felt the call to be a missionary nurse after Dr. Ralph A. Phelps Jr., president of Ouachita Baptist College, spoke at her church, the Second Baptist Church of Little Rock, during the Week of Foreign Missions Emphasis. Not only did she enroll immediately at Ouachita in Arkadelphia, Arkansas, but she became campus nurse there during 1954–56.

Richard attended public school in Berryville up to grade ten, but when his family moved out of town to a ranch, he had no bus or transportation to school. He blazed the way for his younger siblings by attending the School of the Ozarks, at that time a private preparatory boarding school at Point Lookout, Missouri.

From an early age, it was evident that Richard would enter the ministerial field. His friends dubbed him "Deacon Dick," and he lived up to that nickname. Feeling called to the ministry, during his senior year in high school, he organized his friends into a group that preached at the pastorless rural churches.

Richard entered Ouachita as a ministerial student in 1950, but the Korean conflict broke out. He was determined not to follow the example of some of his acquaintances, who had rushed to enroll in seminary training to avoid the armed service. After only one semester, he volunteered for service and, after processing, was sent to Hawaii. It was far from being a paradise as the young recruit underwent rigorous basic training at Schofield Barracks.

After six months, Richard took a test for Officers Command School, but the results of his test were misplaced. When his test results could not be found, he was sent to a noncommissioned leadership school at Fort Jackson, South Carolina. Finally, his test results were located, and he had failed his physical because of curvature of the spine.

He attained the rank of sergeant, but he was not sent to Korea because his records mistakenly showed that he already had a year and a half of overseas service. A stubborn clerk refused to correct the error. After an honorable discharge at the end of two years of service, he again enrolled at Ouachita.

Richard and Bea got off to a rather uncertain start the first time they met in September 1954, but that changed quickly. At that time, Bea had a very sick patient named Frank, so before showering after physical education class, she went by the infirmary to check on him. When she entered the men's ward, she spied a young man sitting on the side of Frank's bed. On the wall beside each bed was a large sign, VISITORS DO NOT SIT ON THE PATIENT'S BED." She quickly reminded the young man of the sign, so he immediately got down and sat in a chair. She checked Frank out and left to get him some juice and to take her shower. As she was going down the hall, she heard footsteps behind her and realized that it was the same young man she had just reprimanded. He introduced himself as Richard Walker, Frank's roommate.

A pep rally around the school's mascot marble tiger was scheduled that evening. Bea walked back into the ward to take care of Frank. While there, she looked around and asked, "Does anyone want to go to the pep rally with me?" Richard always points out that other than himself, there was no one else in the room except Frank, his girlfriend, and another sick patient. Bea doesn't remember those little details.

Richard took her up on the offer, so they went to the pep rally and he walked her home. He now says, "I developed permanent heart trouble." After that evening, he visited Bea at the infirmary every day except when he was out of town. Dr. Phelps gave her special permission to meet Richard after nine at night at the Flenniken Student Center while the campus doctor was visiting the patients at the infirmary during the hours before curfew.

Bea began to realize that she thought a lot of this ministerial student, so she asked him one night, "Has God ever called you to missions?"

Richard thought awhile, then responded, "No, He really hasn't. But—I know that if He should call, I would surrender and go." Bea did not proceed to tell him that she was a mission volunteer but decided instead to wait and let God lead.

Their first date off campus was an unforgettable experience since Richard forgot to take his wallet and Bea paid the bill. On their twenty-fifth wedding anniversary, he pulled out a $50 bill and quipped, "Now the debt is paid in full."

The couple paused one night outside Flenniken Memorial Student Union, and in the light cast by the lamp illuminating the grave marker for John William Conger, Ouachita's founder, Richard proposed. They were married July 1, 1955, at Pleasant Hill Baptist Church in the Sardis community, with the Rev. Dr. Bernes K. Selph performing the ceremony. Bea continued as campus nurse and student, while Richard studied and pastored the First Baptist Church of Amity, some twenty-five miles from Arkadelphia. This was his first pastorate. The two commuted from Amity that fall semester; then she dropped out while he completed his senior year at Ouachita and was graduated in May 1956. Otis Winston, their first son, was born on August 27 of that year.

Winston was only two weeks old when the Walker family moved to Fort Worth, Texas, where Richard enrolled in Southwestern Baptist Theological Seminary. With a car but no money, they borrowed $400 and a trailer to make the move. The money paid for half of one month's rent plus the seminary tuition and necessary books. Before leaving Arkadelphia, they went by Amity where an elderly woman, Mrs. Conine, had wrapped one hundred hard-boiled eggs individually. She also gave them a large amount of canned foods. Bea's mother had given them a case of Pet milk and some jars of Karo syrup for Winston's formula.

Soon after their arrival in Fort Worth, Bea scanned the telephone directory for a Catholic hospital in the area. As she had trained in a Catholic hospital, she felt she would be more comfortable working in one. She found St. Joseph's Hospital, and a telephone call confirmed that there was an opening. She took her application by, but when the supervisor read it, she said, "You must have made a mistake. It says here that you have a three-week-old baby."

Bea assured her that it was not a mistake, so the supervisor told her that the hospital would not hire anyone until six weeks after the birth of a baby and then only after the applicant had been cleared by a physician. She applied three weeks later and was hired. After a year, Bea applied for an opening at the seminary and worked there as a nurse until Richard was graduated.

He worked at odd jobs to support the family for the first few months. With an overabundance of student preachers available to fill nearby pulpits, he was forced to drive two hundred miles one way to minister to a small church, Calvary Baptist, in the community of Nogalus in east Texas. Bea was expected to accompany him to his church. When she became pregnant again, her doctor advised her against making the long trips, but a committee of three elderly deacons objected.

"Preacher, when we hired you, it was understood your wife would come and play the piano. We expect her to be here," they insisted. So she continued to make the grueling trips.

One day Richard came home from classes and found Bea in the kitchen. He put his arms around her waist and asked, "Honey, have you ever thought about being a missionary?"

Bea almost shouted the answer, "Oh, have I? Let me tell you my story!" They sat down and she began to tell him all about what she knew of God's calling and working in her life. She had already begun to pray that God would either remove the desire or call Richard so that they could go together to the mission field.

But the first roadblock to missionary service was encountered in 1958 shortly after Richard had committed to go. A physical examination and X ray required by the Southern Baptist Foreign Mission Board supposedly showed that he, even though he had felt no pain, had an ulcer. The Walkers knew that the Foreign Mission Board would not appoint anyone with an ulcer. Eight weeks later, another X ray revealed no scar, but Richard was still not given clearance for the mission field.

He completed his work at the seminary and was called in 1959 as pastor of the First Baptist Church of Hammon, Oklahoma. William Boyd, their second son, was born October 18, 1959. In 1962, Richard became pastor of Northwest Baptist Church of Atlanta, Georgia.

Each year for five years, and at his own expense, Richard had been X-rayed, and each time no ulcer was found. Each year the results were sent to the Foreign Mission Board. Finally, in the fifth year, the board decided that either there was a flaw on the first X-ray film or the film had been mixed with someone else's and had been labeled with Richard's name. The couple was finally appointed on July 16, 1964, for overseas service. Again, Bea's mother voiced an objection, "If only you didn't have small children . . ."

Chapter 2

The Walkers sailed from New Orleans on the steamship *Del Sud* on August 19, 1964, and after nearly three weeks at sea, saw Brazil for the first time on September 4. Assigned to Campinas, São Paulo, they studied the Portuguese language at the Escola de Português e Orientação (School of Portuguese and Orientation) through August 1965.

Bea soon found that lack of knowledge of the language could prove a bit embarrassing. After only a few days in language school, the Walkers were visited by three men from the Campinas church. Although she did not understand anything they said, she smiled and bowed each time conversation was addressed to her.

Later, the family attended church services, but waited in vain for the service to begin. Finally, one of the other missionaries approached and inquired, "Bea, aren't you supposed to play the piano?" Unknowingly, she had agreed to serve as pianist when she smiled her assent to the three-man church committee! Richard now confesses that he was totally unaware for months that his Brazilian neighbor stuttered.

Once the Walkers watched proudly as young Boyd rattled on in Portuguese. They were brought up short, however, when a girl came over and asked, "Do you know what Boyd is saying? He is talking ugly."

Boyd came in crying after a neighborhood boy had hit him.

"Did you do anything to cause him to strike you?" Richard inquired.

"No, he just hit me," Boyd wailed.

Older brother Winston then arrived and jibed at Boyd, "Guess you'll never call him a *monkey* again!"

Both Winston and Boyd attended a Brazilian school in Campinas. In the afternoon a Brazilian tutor would come in to help them with their homework, since Bea did not yet know Portuguese well enough to help them.

Although a handicap, Richard's lack of command of the Portuguese language did not sideline him. After his first sermon in January, he preached eighty-two times during the first year, reading his sermons in Portuguese, with ninety-seven professions of faith being made then. He was also asked by a national pastor to baptize four persons while in Campinas.

After six months in language school, he, along with two fellow Arkansans, Glenn Hickey and James Wilson, set out in a Jeep station wagon on a one-week preaching mission to Jacupiranga, some two hundred miles south of São Paulo. They would also preach at churches in Lavras and Guaraú, approximately thirty kilometers from Jacupiranga and from each other.

The three were housed in the Palace Hotel in Jacupiranga, but their "palatial" quarters consisted of a seven-foot by twelve-foot room, with three bunk beds and four nails on which to hang their clothes. The "bathroom" had no hot water, soap, or toilet paper.

Both Lavras and Guaraú were six miles off the main highway on almost impassable routes that included crossing a river. The Jeep drowned out several times and became stuck on other occasions, but the missionaries remained undaunted. Neither rural church had electricity nor other modern facilities, but the membership remained dedicated to their Lord's service.

At Lavras a sanctuary crowded with 250 persons greeted the missionaries each night from Wednesday through Sunday. Twenty-four accepted Christ as their personal Savior. In addition, the trio preached on Sunday afternoon in a steady sprinkle to a crowd of two hundred in the yard of a Christian's home six kilometers from Lavras. Twelve of those attending made professions of faith.

The Lavras church consistently had 180 in Sunday school. A few years before, when it had been the only church in the area, its members had met at the church *every night* for two years to pray for the needs of the people and for their own responsibility to show the light of Christ. Richard notes that no one at Lavras, except the missionaries, came to services by car or truck, but walked or rode horses or bicycles.

In Guaraú the group had twelve conversions even though it missed two services because of the roads and inclement weather.

In Jacupiranga, the trio recorded nineteen conversions for a total of seventy-nine. Richard preached twice a day most of the time and four times on Sunday. Once, while traveling by horseback to a preaching point nearly two hours from Lavras, he and his saddle toppled to the ground as the saddle girth broke while the horse was ascending a steep hill or mountain. Fortunately, none of his bones were broken.

As the missionaries had been in language school for only six months, they had prepared only three sermons each and could not deliver them in Portuguese without reading them. They constantly exchanged pulpits in order to keep their sermons "fresh."

Laymen led many of the worship services in the churches of the area. Joaquim Aguiar Severo was not only pastor at Lavras, with 180 in Sunday school, but also at Jacupiranga, with 235 in Sunday school, and at Cajatí. Despite being a cripple with an old bicycle as his only means of transportation, he was happy in the service of his Lord.

As part of the Great National Campaign of Evangelization of 1965 conducted by Baptists, Richard and his two cohorts had helped to stem a divergent religious movement that had caused dissension in the churches. The members now began to practice personal evangelization, and many excluded members were reclaimed.

Despite all their difficulties on the mission trip, the trio still probably had it comparatively easy compared to some of the early pioneers who, as early as 1925, had established Baptist churches in the area known as "Vale do Ribeiro," sometimes called "the Baptist Valley." One of these was Dr. A. B. Deter, a huge man weighing more than 230 pounds, with one leg shorter than the other. It was difficult for Dr. Deter to ride a horse, but when news that he was coming arrived, twelve to fifteen strong men from Lavras would volunteer to carry him. Some went to Jacupiranga and took a boat by night up the river.

After rowing all night and into the day, they would arrive at the port of Manoel Gomes. Dr. Deter would lie down in a hanging bed; and carrying it on their backs, four men in shifts would ascend and descend the mountains and cross rivers for some twenty kilometers to Lavras.

On Saturday, May 29, 1965, Ronnie Boswell, a personal friend and fellow language student, came by to ask Richard to preach for him at a small church in the small town of Valinhos near Campinas. He said that he had another engagement, then added with a laugh, "Besides, I have already been to Valinhos."

Richard was glad to get a chance to preach, so he loaded his entire family into a borrowed car and headed for Valinhos on Sunday. The small Baptist church in the pretty and clean little town was crowded with people, most of whom had a *sackola,* or shopping bag, filled with merchandise or ready for shopping after the service.

Bea thought she had never heard a noisier crowd. The people walked around and continued to talk as the service began, while babies kept up their wailing. In addition, noisy trucks roared by on the street in front of the church. Midway through Richard's sermon, however, Bea noticed that a sudden quiet settled over the crowd. The babies quit their crying. She no longer heard the noise of the trucks. At the end of the service, seven adults accepted Christ as their Savior. She now knew why Ronnie had said, "I have already been to Valinhos."

Chapter 3

The Walkers were getting anxious to get to the Amazon. They didn't know where they would work, but just before they finished language school, they took a field trip and visited every station where Southern Baptists had missionaries in equatorial Brazil. Richard and Bea were excited by their trip and decided that they could work at any of these places.

Bea had not prayed much about the last place they had visited since the request was for an itinerant river ministry. She felt that surely God would not call them to a river ministry because she did not like water and could not swim. Richard knew nothing of boats, and while eight of his brothers had served in some branch of the Navy, he alone had served as an infantryman. They found out, however, that God did have a sense of humor since He called the *infantryman* to the river ministry!

They were landing at the airport in Manaus, a thousand miles up the Amazon from the coast, and viewed all the lights of the city. They looked at each other at the same time and said, "This is it." There was a finality to the decision, for they felt that God had spoken and they need not look further. They stayed in Manaus for several days, visited the Second Baptist Church, and traveled out on the river. They then returned to Campinas to finish the year of language school.

In a letter dated June 30, 1965, Richard was invited while still in Campinas to become pastor of the Second Baptist Church of Manaus. He wrote a letter of acceptance in Portuguese on July 8, cautioning however that he would not be able to preach at the church every week because he would be ministering to other churches, which he could reach only by boat. In a formal ceremony on Sunday morning, September 19, he was installed as pastor of the church, which had only 45 members, although it was 45 years old.

Bea would be very active here, pumping the old organ for some years until they were able to take back a new electronic organ from the States. She also would work with the Women's Missionary Union and the Young Women's Auxiliary.

There were two other missionary couples and two single female missionaries in Manaus at the time. Sid and Ruth Carswell, with their four children, had been in Manaus for a year, while Lonnie and Janell Doyle, with five children, had been in Manaus for twelve years. Ona Belle Cox was in charge of the Baptist school, while Dorothy Latham directed the Good Will Center.

The Walkers soon became close friends of Moacyr and Eunice Alves, a very prominent couple in the town. Most of their social life revolved around their relationship with this couple. Moacyr was a lawyer.

After Richard had preached several times, Moacyr told him, "Pastor, why don't you throw your manuscript away? After all, you converse well in Portuguese, and I think you could do well with just an outline."

"Well, friend, if I just have an outline, it won't take me long to get through the sermon," Richard protested.

"I will help you," Moacyr replied. After that, as the song director, he would sit on Richard's left behind the pulpit and never take his eyes off the preacher. When Richard came to unfamiliar territory in Portuguese, he would turn to Moacyr, who would give him a word or two, and he would continue preaching.

While at Campinas, Winston and Boyd had studied in a Portuguese school and had a tutor to help them with their homework. The two boys learned the language quickly. After arrival at Manaus, they enrolled in the Ida Nelson Baptist School, which had been built with missionary funds and had more than 400 students, ranging from kindergarten through Grade 12. They continued in Brazilian schools up to high school.

During the afternoon, Bea taught them their lessons in English, using the Calvert method so that they would be able to compete with their age group when they were on furlough in the United States. She spent four hours each day since she had to teach Winston in one grade and Boyd in another.

As she had not been trained as a teacher, Bea worried about what effect her teaching might have on her children and whether they would resent her later. Instead, they became avid advocates of missionaries' instructional methods, enrolling their children in the Brazilian schools and letting them relate well to the Brazilians while assuring English education using their mother's methods.

The Walkers emphasize that they did not initiate the Amazon River ministry. Eric Nelson, the pioneer Baptist missionary to Amazonas, had established many churches and had died in Manaus on June 17, 1939, after thirty-eight years of arduous service. Richard was determined to help rebuild these churches and to establish new work.

His passionate desire was to preach the gospel to those who had never heard it. This was facilitated by funds from the Southern Baptist annual Lottie Moon Foreign Mission offering that had earlier purchased a 42-foot cabin cruiser with a 50-horse power motor. Named the *Eurico Nelson,* it carried tanks on top storing water for kitchen and shower use in order to avoid the flesh-eating piranha in the river. It contained two bunks and places for several hammocks to hang. It had a capacity for enough diesel fuel to last 85 to 90 hours, and it could travel fifteen miles per hour upstream.

Accompanied by fellow missionary Sid Carswell, Richard set out in October 1965 on his first river trip, and after five days arrived at the little village of Vila Fernandes. No evangelical service had ever been held there, although some in the crowd had attended a Baptist church at one time or another. He preached on the love of God from John 13:1–5. When the invitation was given, everyone in the audience above the age of fourteen, about twenty in number, accepted Christ as Savior and stood before the group to give testimony of their faith.

On the return trip, the two missionaries stopped at the home of a believer at a site where there was formerly a Baptist church. No one had been there, however, to help the congregation for several years. They noticed that someone had bought tile to cover the small building. After questioning Adam, the believer in whose home they had stopped, they found that he had bought the tile even though he made less than a dollar a week, lived one hundred miles by river from the nearest town, and had only a canoe for travel.

"God is not going to let me die until our church is living again," Adam declared. The missionaries held a prayer meeting in Adam's home.

As they headed for home, they were temporarily stalled when the starter for their boat broke. Rather than be pulled the four hundred miles back to Manaus, they decided to hitch a ride. Never one to miss an opportunity to preach the gospel, Richard asked the captain of the rather large boat that was pulling them for permission to hold a service on board. The captain agreed and the missionary preached at nine o'clock the next morning from John 3, with five professions of faith.

Not long after that, while reading his Bible in Portuguese, Winston decided to accept Christ as his Savior. His father baptized him in the Manaus Second Baptist Church water tank.

Chapter 4

Just what kind of people did the Walkers find among these hardy residents along the Amazon and its many tributaries? How did they live?

They were to find that the people were a mixture of three ethnic groups: Portuguese, whites who came from Portugal in 1500 when the Portuguese founded the country of Brazil; Indians who were there when the Portuguese arrived; and blacks, either slaves whom the Portuguese brought from Africa, or former slaves who migrated to the Amazon valley after the War between the States. In addition, some white ex-Confederate soldiers migrated with their families to the valley after the War between the States.

Typical Brazilians are very beautiful people, with olive skin, black hair, and very dark eyes. They speak Portuguese, but the Indian tribes speak their own dialects and are shielded by the Brazilian government, which allows no one to go near them. The Indians are hostile to those not of their own kind and even in recent years have killed those who dared to go near them.

For other Brazilians, the dress is typical Western wear, but for those in the interior, their supply is limited and ready-made clothes are expensive. Merchants from town carry fabrics and other wares by boat. These are expensive, but this is the only way for those in the interior to obtain something new. Usually someone in the village sews for others. The Walkers soon began to urge visitors to bring good, used clothing, especially for children, when they made mission trips to the Amazon. These were distributed and well received.

It was a mystery to the Walkers how these river people managed to subsist. None of them receive a minimum wage, even though that is usually only $30 a month. They might sell a fish, farinha that the family made, a chicken, a pig, or even a cow.

Three crops make up their sources of income. One of these is Brazil nuts, which the men and boys gather from the jungle. Another

This straw-thatched house might be considered one of the better dwelling houses among the people who live in the Amazon Basin.

is rubber. The tall softwood tree, native to Brazil, is cut much the same way that maple trees are cut to catch the sap. The milky liquid or latex found in the inner bark is then coagulated by being heated over a clay furnace burning homemade charcoal. The coagulated rubber is sold to the river merchants who take it to town for export.

The third money crop is jute, which grows naturally. The Brazilians cut it when the jute is mature and leave it in the river for several days. They then flail the jute floating on top of the water to remove the bark, then hang it on lines to dry. After it is thoroughly dry, the workers roll it into bales and sell it to merchants for export. Burlap used for carpet backs and ropes is one of the products from jute.

The river people's diet consists of fish caught daily, a coarse meal called farinha made from the manioc root, bananas, an apple substitute called jumbo, oranges, papaya, pineapple, mango, and other fruits. They do little farming or gardening, but some plant their gardens close to the river's edge with the knowledge that they will harvest their crop before the river rises too much. They may raise corn, beans, green peppers, green onions, cabbage, and black pepper. When able, they purchase rice and coffee, and occasionally dried beans. They get sugarcane from the jungle.

The farinha, which the river people put all over their food, is made by individual families. The root of the manioc bush is fatally poisonous to a cow or other animal eating it. The people, however, take the root of the manioc bush, soak it, peel off the bark, put it in a tipiti, and squeeze the juice out of it. The tipiti is a cylinder of the jacitara palm used to extract the poisonous juice.

They then grind it up, and after greasing a large pan with a fresh Brazil nut, put it over a fire in a clay oven with a hole in it, and constantly stir it until it is completely dry and ready for use. Richard thought it tasted like a cross between a rock and sawdust, but Bea, like the Brazilians, thought it was delicious.

Another common food preparation method is the piracaia. In the procedure, sticks are gathered and set on fire. Fish is cooked on this open fire. Bea thought that perhaps our exotic blackened fish dishes began this way.

Unless one lives only a short distance away, no one commutes to Manaus. A majority of the people who live along the river never get very close to town, and many live their lives within a small radius from their birthplaces.

The typical home along the river is made very simply of adobe, thatch, or wood. A home with thatch roof and three or four sides also made of thatch is not uncommon. Many homes have dirt floors, but they are swept clean. These thatch homes have a wooden frame, and if constructed properly, they seldom leak. Hammocks are folded or rolled up in a ball and left hanging on a nail during the daytime. There may or may not be a roughly hewn table. Bales of jute or baskets made of banana leaves filled with farinha are the "chairs."

The kitchen is usually a lean-to covered with thatch. All of the cooking is done here and most will have a homemade clay oven. The river people have a couple of aluminum pans, and their homemade soaps make these pans shine. Such articles are carried to the river for washing. Most of the women throw out waste water and randomly it stands where it hits, often making it a hog wallow. The Walkers were unsuccessful in encouraging them to dig a hole and fill it with rocks to eliminate standing water, thus making their surroundings more healthful.

Usually a house will have two rooms plus the lean-to. Many live in each house, normally a dozen or more. People who can't even feed their own will take in a baby or young child who needs a home, whether it's a relative or not, and will bring that child up as their own. Usually children, parents, grandparents, and at times, an uncle and aunt, will live in one small house.

While most houses are located on the riverbank, many are built and placed on and tied to logs. These *flutuantes* are floating houses. If too many people crowd into a house, water comes over the logs and into the house. This causes the tremendous problem of the anaconda, the water boa constrictor, which is sometimes found in the house. Another problem is the piranha, the flesh-eating fish. Scraps are thrown into the water and cause a danger to small children as schools of piranha gather to eat the scraps. However, both Richard and Bea have survived falls into the river, and he has conducted baptisms in the rivers.

The temperature is quite uncomfortable within the homes since this is the rainforest, only 3 degrees south of the equator. The people close up their windows just before dusk because this is the time when the mosquitoes swarm. The only lamp is a lamparina made from a type of oil can. They pour kerosene into this and have a little rag for a wick. When it is lit, it gives off more smoke than light. The more affluent homes have several lamparinas.

Dogs and cats—generally skinny, mangy, and unhealthy looking—are always present. In addition, the river people raise chickens, pigs, and perhaps a cow. The problem with raising a cow is that the river rises six months out of the year, flooding the land so that there is no place to keep the cow. Regardless of the rainfall, if the river is going down, it will continue to go down. If it is rising, it will continue to rise regardless of how dry it is. Evidently, conditions of the snow in the Andes Mountains control the rising and falling of the river.

Many different kinds of wild game abound in the jungle. Wild hogs, running in packs, are extremely dangerous but good to eat. The Walkers found the cutia, a rodent, to be delicious. The capivara is the world's largest rodent and is very good to eat. Some eat monkey and a variety of ducks and other birds.

The Walkers found it difficult to protect themselves from mosquitoes. Like other Americans, they owned mosquito nets, but found them to be hot, making sleeping almost impossible. Native Brazilians rarely have access to this luxury.

Every one of the river people seemed to have a history of malaria, and occasionally there were isolated cases of yellow fever. The government sends boats up the river to spray the homes in attempts to control malaria.

Medical facilities are unheard of very far from town. Many people live a lifetime and never see a doctor or dentist. Rabies is not at all rare, and it is not uncommon to read in the newspapers of Manaus or Santarém that someone has died of this horrible disease. Richard and Bea longed for the day when as many as possible of these people would have an opportunity to see a doctor or a dentist at least *once* in their lifetimes.

The river is the very life blood of the people. It is their means of transportation, their only contact with the outside world. From it comes their food and their drink, their water for crops. Life is very difficult for anyone not living along a river, creek, or stream.

Baths are taken in the river. The women take a bath with their clothes on. After the bath, they dip their pails into the water so that they can take home their drinking water. Some take what is called a "cuia" bath in a canoe. A cuia is a gourd, and when cut in half becomes a bowl. After soaping up, the person fills the cuia with water and pours it over the head and body. Then the cuia is used as a bowl for eating.

All drinking water comes from the river. In addition to using the river water for drinking and taking baths, it is carried by people of all ages to the house to be used for laundry, washing dishes, and bathing pets.

Although education is gradually becoming more accessible, the farther the missionary couple got from the cities, the fewer schools they found. School in their river ministry area is not compulsory, but more and more are attending classes for two or three years and adults are attending special night classes. This is a big help in stamping out illiteracy. More and more villages provide classes for the first three years, but government-employed teachers go for months at a time without pay. The many schools in the larger cities include law school and medical school, as well as schools to train elementary and high school teachers.

These are the people of the Amazon among whom the Walkers would minister for ten years. They spoke their Portuguese language, coped with their primitive ways, and ministered to their spiritual and physical needs whenever possible.

They adapted themselves to differences between church life in Manaus and that along the river. In Manaus the Sunday morning services are little more than the Sunday school and a devotional time. The people dress casually for the morning service, but dress up for the night service, which is usually a mixture of singing accompanied by guitars and organ and evangelistic preaching. The pastor usually asks to see the hands of the non-Christians, who lift their hands unashamedly.

The rural or interior Christians leave their flip-flop shoes at the door of the church since they are usually muddy. The people are very proud of their church building and do not want to make it dirty. Most of their pews are backless and cushionless, but the people sit for long hours and seem to enjoy the long periods of time. They are simply glad to be together.

The interior people are simple and honest. In Anamã, where Boyd would soon accept Christ, Richard preached in a home, and afterward a man approached him and said that he wanted a Bible. Richard explained that he didn't have any more Bibles this trip. However, he said he would leave his personal Bible with the man and would bring him one when he returned to the village.

A few weeks later, Richard and his entire family returned with a paper-bound New Testament. The man wanted one just like the missionary's—a leather-bound one with zipper.

He was told that it was a very expensive Bible and the American couldn't afford to give it away. The persistent man said he would pay for the Bible. At that, Richard promised to bring him one on the next trip, but he would leave the paper-bound one for now.

Later in the afternoon, the man ran toward the boat and yelled, "Pastor Richard! Pastor Richard! I don't need the leather-bound Bible."

Richard questioned him for his reason, as he had been so insistent.

He held up the paper-bound New Testament with a large portion separated from the rest.

"I've read this much of this one, and it has the same thing as yours does. I don't need the expensive one after all."

On the same trip, Richard, Bea, and the boys stopped at dusk to share with a man and his entire family at a house near the bend of the river where boats cross the larger expanse to hug the river bank and avoid the channel as they went upstream. It was called Travesia.

This home was unusual in that it had a table with benches to sit on. As everyone sat around the table and Richard preached, the man of the house kept saying out loud, "That's the way I thought it ought to be." He, his wife, and three of his older children made decisions for Christ that very hour.

Chapter 5

Richard, accompanied by his cabin boy, Heraclides, would make another of his many trips into this primitive river world when on December 1 of that same year, 1965, he decided to revisit Vila Fernandes in addition to stopping at other places en route. While going up river, they kept close to the bank to avoid the current of the river. Even though he arrived at the Island of Patience later than he had promised, he was able to preach to some thirty adults who had never heard the Gospel preached in an evangelical manner.

Leaving the island at 10:00 P.M. they traveled all night. In fact, except for stopping because of the threat of a storm or because it was too dark to navigate, they continued up river for forty-nine hours. Many times Richard longed to stop at places he saw along the bank, but he knew that he could not do so and accomplish his stated mission.

He wrote in his diary: "The people are hungry. You can see it as you preach. They listen as though it were a matter of Life or Death, and truly it is. And you have such a short time to tell them so much."

After leaving the Island of Patience on Wednesday night, they arrived in the little town of Coari, a short distance from Fernandes, late Friday night. On Saturday morning, when the governor on the fuel injection pump for the boat would not work, Richard left Heraclides to repair the boat while he put his 14-horsepower Evinrude motor on a rented canoe and headed upriver toward Fernandes.

After only twenty minutes, the Evinrude began to cut out, to sputter and stop, so he returned to the boat. After trying to repair the governor on the boat for three hours, he knelt beside the injector pump and prayed, "Lord, this is Your trip. I am here only because You sent me. I would greatly desire to finish the trip and the preaching planned. If this is Your desire, then You will have to fix this injector pump. If You do not, I will get a tow down river back home."

After praying, he turned the key, the engine started, and they finished the trip without further problems.

This and many other occasions taught the missionary to rely 100 percent upon the Lord for that which seemed impossible. He found that God calmed the storms, stopped the rain, and intervened in the lives of people and animals. God repaired more than one boat and led through many dark nights when the moon and stars were hidden.

The "crew" arrived in Vila Fernandes at 9:00 P.M. on Saturday, finding that the people had heard over the radio that they would stay several days. They found the twenty who had made decisions before still happy in their newfound faith. In services through Tuesday, nineteen more made decisions.

During this time, Richard found that he had less zeal for fishing for fish than for men. He was unsuccessful in thirty minutes of fishing and in hunting for duck, but found five families living on the lake near Vila Fernandes. He preached to them, with five conversions.

Richard continued to preach on the trip back down river and stopped at the church where Adam had bought the tile. Here he held services at the church in the afternoon and at night on Big Catuá Island in the home of one of the members of the church. There were no decisions, but those on the island agreed to come to Adam's house the next afternoon for services. Richard gave a man some gasoline for his small boat and he agreed to bring them.

When a storm prevented the small boat from crossing over from the island, Richard went after them in his larger boat. This time there were eight decisions for Christ. At the conclusion of the two-week trip, he had preached at eleven different locations, with 79 accepting Christ as their Savior. Multiple services were conducted at some of the places, with José, a Brazilian, preaching twice.

The Walkers were homesick for the States as they spent their second Christmas season in Brazil. They thought of their friends enduring cold weather, but cheered by sitting around a warm fire. They knew that back in the States their loved ones would be doing last-minute shopping, busying themselves with school activities, or practicing for the Christmas cantata.

In Manaus, Christmas meant a bit cooler weather of perhaps 82 to 90 degrees, more rain with the river rising, with only a few stores having Christmas decorations. The missionaries would decorate their homes in the traditional American style, and there would be an all-church Christmas program. Instead of building a snowman, the children would try to catch one of the hundreds of parakeets, or play with "Chiquinha da Silva," a little monkey Richard had brought home from his last trip. The children would also gather a few mangos, a very delicious fruit, and sell them to a vendor who came by to purchase them. But the Walkers knew that for everyone the world over, Christmas meant Jesus, salvation, hope, and life.

Richard would make many more river trips into the interior to revisit the churches and to seek out places where the Gospel had never been preached. In a report in Portuguese to the thirty-fifth annual Amazonas State Baptist Convention covering only from September 1965 to February 1966, he listed that he had preached 38 times, with 141 decisions.

All was not rosy, he confided to Steve Philpot, a preacher friend in Dallas, on April 12, 1966. Entitled "From a wilderness of jungle, water, and beasts; from a desert of spiritual poverty and problems; from a field full and overflowing and white unto harvest and some over-ripe," he wrote of contention in his church at Manaus. Established by Eric Nelson forty-five years ago, the Second Baptist Church of Manaus still had only forty-five members and had never started another preaching point, nor another mission nor church.

Although he was able to spend only half of his time at the church, Richard had preached and visited individually among the members in an effort to stop the backbiting and acrimony among the membership. He noted that this was not the type of thing missionaries related in order to raise money for the Lottie Moon Christmas offering for foreign missions.

Richard was more enthusiastic in telling his Dallas friend about his 600-mile round trip to revisit Vila Fernandes and other preaching points from February 27 to March 10. He had left the work at Fernandes in the hands of a baptized believer of one year. Richard was heartened to discover that services had been held regularly since he had been there in October, with about fifty in attendance.

It was here that he discovered that the bushing around the drive shaft of the boat propeller had worn out and had fallen out. This meant that each time they stopped, Heraclides, the cabin boy, had to swim under the boat and put something around the drive shaft to keep water out of the boat.

At each stop, Richard would ask about the health of the people. He had with him medicine for malaria and eye infections. People were eager for the medicine since they had to pay high prices for medicine sold by river peddlers. In addition to the medicine, the missionary also gave out free Bibles and hymn books as fast as he could. He brought along candy for the children, some of whom also sought the crackers he had brought for himself as a substitute for bread. He began to wonder how long he could afford the extra expense.

In return, the people would give graciously from what they had. Surprises were often in store for Richard when the people gave him meat of unknown origin. After he had attempted to answer one man's questions about the Scripture he had used in a service, Richard was invited to his house and offered a slice of meat from an agouti, an animal about the size of a rabbit and related to the guinea pig.

He knew that he could not lie if the man asked him what he thought about it, but fortunately he found that it was tender and tasted like the breast of a fryer. Once he was given a fillet from a sea cow that was as tender as the tenderloin of a hog, but tasted like beef.

Although they had to pump water out of the boat every half hour during the last part of the trip, he and his boat boy arrived back in Manaus at 7:00 A.M. on March 10. It was Richard's birthday, and Bea greeted him with a cake she had baked.

Chapter 6

Winston and Boyd made their first trip into the interior with their father in April 1966. The two boys caught a large number of small, flesh-eating piranha, known for their voracity. A school of piranha is capable of devouring a steer, or man, in ten minutes, but normally they do not attack unless they smell blood. Richard removed the piranha from the hooks, but mistook one of the smaller ones for a perch. It leaped two inches and bit off a small part of his thumb.

His ministry was mainly for adults, and until now adults were the only ones who had made professions of faith. On this trip, however, three children and an eighteen-year-old girl accepted Christ at Costa do Louro, the first persons to do so in this location. The people here supplied six stalks of bananas, a large duck, and offered chicken if Richard and the boys were unsuccessful at fishing.

On the last day of the April trip, they were on a lake surrounded by black water, an area that Richard described as the most beautiful place he had seen in Amazonas. He preached at a place where the people were gathering Brazil nuts. Although the crowd was noisy, there were eleven professions of faith.

After they got back into the boat, Boyd said, "Daddy, I raised my hand tonight."

"Why?" Richard asked his son, who was only six and a half years old.

"To accept Jesus as my Savior," Boyd replied.

Richard talked to his son and was convinced that the lad knew what he was doing. The father delayed baptism, however, until they could be home on furlough because of the Brazilian Baptist attitude against baptizing young children.

In May, Richard made a trip upriver with fellow missionary Jim Wilson. Concerning the night of May 9, he wrote:

The night was beautifully clear and was more filled with stars than I ever remember seeing it before. Jim and I lay on top of the boat, looking and talking. It surely makes me feel small when looking at God's great universe. Again, it makes me to know anew the greatness of God's love. Amongst all the hosts of heavenly bodies, we saw one little dim satellite streak out across the sky. If anyone was in it, he still had to look *up* to see God's handiwork.

And to think, man who boasts so of making that lone, little, dim, temporary satellite, also boasts himself against God and has the gall to ask, "Is God dead?" A star just shot across the sky much faster, brighter, and more beautifully than our little man-made speck. How grateful and humbled I am to KNOW that in this vast universe, God knows where we are tonight. He, too, rejoices at the repentance of one sinner and *wants* more than we the salvation of every individual on this great river. He watches over us all and blesses the preaching of the Word. What more could we want?

Jim's leg became swollen and infected from a bug bite, so they hurried back toward Manaus. They arrived in Betania a day early and were met by a man who said he had gotten his documents in order and was now legally married. He wanted Richard, however, to perform a marriage ceremony for them. The couple had been living together for fourteen years and had five children.

Although he had left his pastor's manual at home, Richard performed his first marriage in Portuguese for the couple. He was dressed in khakis, sports shirt, and boots, while the bride held a baby in her arms throughout the service. There was no music.

The boat attracted many curious spectators, and Richard often awoke to find people staring in the windows at them or the boat. At one location, he was offered a blond-haired girl for adoption, and two other small girls begged their parents to be allowed to go with the missionary and be his children. He found that families were often willing to give up their children so that the children might have a better lifestyle in a missionary's home.

By July 1966, he had made four 1,000-mile round trips of two weeks duration each, six trips of one or two days each to areas where there were no churches, three weekend trips to nearby churches, and one six-day trip to a new area. He recorded at least 286 professions of faith and 18 baptisms. Two new churches were established.

Unless she accompanied him, Bea had no contact with him or

he with her until he returned to Manaus as there were no telephones in the interior. This would be true during the ten years that he ministered in Manaus, but more and more limited telephone services are now available in the remote areas.

It was not until a year after Richard had made his first river trip that Bea was able to accompany him. Her responsibilities in the local church and the teaching of Winston and Boyd had prevented this. The trip in October 1966 got off to a rocky start, for after only seventy minutes, the boat's exhaust got too hot. They stopped in the middle of the river to repair it, but then the starter wouldn't work.

Maneuvering the heavy boat to shore, Richard and Heraclides tried in vain to repair the starter. Finally, Heraclides went to find some missionaries nearby at the school operated by New Tribes Mission. They pulled the boat back to the school, but a mechanic there was unable to get it started. Heraclides took the starter back to Manaus for repairs.

After beginning their voyage again, Richard discovered that they had lost half their diesel fuel, so they had to operate with only half power. They finally arrived at their first destination, Itacotiara, at 2:15 A.M. The message that they were coming had not been delivered, so a layman from Manaus had been invited to preach that morning. Richard would not stay as he said there were too many places with no witness for two ministers to remain in one service.

Instead, they took off to the house of Heraclides' mother and arrived there that afternoon. Heraclides spread the word that services would be held at 3:00 P.M. at the home of a believer. Bea noted that both the house and yard were full of people and mosquitoes. A very drunk man tried to stand directly in front of Richard, but despite this, twenty-four adults made professions of faith. Another service was held at 7:00 P.M. at the home of Heraclides' mother, with fourteen making decisions for Christ.

Finding themselves on the river on October 17, a day before Boyd's seventh birthday, they decided to celebrate a day early with the chocolate cake they had brought, along with some frosting sent from the United States.

Later, unable to find a man they were looking for, they stopped in a beautiful lake to fish. Each caught at least one piranha. Bea wrote in the diary: "After dark Richard shined the lights of the boat on the river bank and there were *many* alligator eyes! Made me feel a bit 'creepy.' We tied up for the night at 11:45 P.M. I felt quite safe even though we were in alligator-infested waters because we locked the door—leaving the key in the door outside! I don't suppose the alligators would have tried to unlock the door, *BUT* I've heard all about the river thieves."

The five hours that Richard had spent fishing during this fifteen-day trip were enough to give him the fishing bug. As Manaus was near the best fishing location in the world, he decided to make an overnight fishing trip. Taking his friend Moacyr Alves with him, he journeyed to the spot some one and a half hours from Manaus.

He baited Moacyr's hook and the lawyer, who was not accustomed to fishing, was delighted to pull in a large catfish. Richard was slower in having success, but after getting many nibbles, he finally got a strike. After reeling out about five yards of line, he set his hook and was almost pulled into the waters from the rocks he was standing on. He jumped into the canoe and finally reeled in a huge catfish estimated to weigh at least eighty-five pounds. Heraclides killed it with a knife. They decided to take only the fillet part, but that alone weighed thirty-five pounds. Because of the abundance of other fish available to the Brazilians, they ignore catfish, which only the Americans will eat.

Bea had managed to stay in the background of much of the church work, especially anything involving controversy. This was not to last, however, after she was elected to serve as a messenger from the Second Baptist Church to the Baptist State Convention of Amazonas held at Memorial Church in Manaus from January 4 to 10, 1967. Pastor Antunes Oliveira, long-time criticizer of missionaries, was elected as president. When he named the Committee on Committees, he made Bea chairman. As she was sitting in the back of the room, she was too timid to speak up and demur.

Despite feeling her inadequacy, she called a meeting of the committee immediately, and with the help of her good friend Eunice Alves, managed to get through the session quite well. She had another successful meeting at her home the following day.

At the convention that night, however, there was heated discussion about two names on the state board. Finally, against her protests, the committee replaced those two names with those of Bea and another younger person. When the names of all proposed members were read at the convention, Pastor Miguel Horvath arose to say that two members of the committee were too inexperienced. Bea knew to whom he was referring.

Finally, a motion was made that her name be stricken from the committee. When the debate became even more heated, the Walkers left for home. The next day, a conciliatory group came to their home, and even Pastor Artunes, who had never before been known to apologize, made a long speech. Bea was emotionally drained and remained in her room much of the next day. Then two men from the committee visited her later in the day and encouraged her greatly.

The long rides up river could become boring, as evidenced from an entry in the diary for a trip up the Rio Solimões from February 3 to 12, 1967. The following entry was made by ten-year-old Winston: "Monday we drove all morning, all afternoon and all night. Daddy wouldn't let me drive because we were going up river and had to stay close to the bank. We hardly did anything but drive, cook and wash dishes. My job was to wash dishes."

Winston found it more interesting ashore. At one preaching point, he wrote: "As Daddy was waiting for some people to come, I went around the back of the house. I saw a Papagaio (black parrot). They wanted to give it to us because it was chewing their palha (straw) and they did not want to kill it because it was so pretty and so they gave it to us as a present."

As happened so often, boat problems delayed the trip. Winston wrote that the brakes wouldn't work, water was coming into the boat, and the boat would not go backwards.

In March, Richard took a two-week trip by airplane to Pôrto Velho and Guajará Mirím in the federal territory of Rôndonia. While there, he traveled both by car and bicycle.

He would take the final river trip of his first mission tour from May 22 to June 2, 1967, before going back to the United States for a year of furlough. Filemon Pereira da Silva, who would work in the river ministry while they were on furlough, planned to make the trip but did not arrive on time. After waiting as long as he could, Richard decided to proceed without him.

The trip started off with boat difficulties as the muffler inside the boat broke after two days of travel. For the next two days, they were covered with smoke and soot and had to return to Manaus to make repairs. There sat Filemon waiting for them. God had used a broken exhaust to send them back for the young preacher.

In addition, they had lost a trailing canoe, but found it later at the little town of Codajãs. A man there had seen it out in the river, had pulled it ashore, and had kept it for Richard. On his first day out, he set out to look for things that were different. He saw some monkeys, usually scared into the jungle by the sound of the boat motor, playing in trees along the bank. Some were little red ones that were not very easy to tame.

Birds of many species were in abundance. Among these were many parakeets, parrots, and macaws (which Richard often referred to as parrots). He noticed that parrots flew in pairs, with those predominantly red never mixing with those that were predominantly blue. He observed a boat loading cattle for market in Manaus. One cow had broken loose and was being pursued by men in a canoe. The river was at its crest, and only the roofs of some houses stood above water.

The great height of the water caused the baptism on this trip to be unusual. Richard walked down the steps of a house and performed the ceremony from there. The people either stood on logs or walkways made by the owner, or looked on from the windows of their houses. There was no yard in which to stand.

Fishing was good on this trip. Catfish up to one hundred pounds were caught, along with tucunaré, a type of bass weighing from fifteen to twenty pounds. Some small fish even jumped into the boat as it ran through a school.

Despite being gone from his home church in Manaus often, he progressed well with the work at the Second Baptist Church. Its membership doubled and through money received from the Lottie Moon Foreign Mission offering a new sanctuary costing some $7,000 was built.

A special service was held on June 10, 1967, to dedicate the new sanctuary and to begin a revival meeting. Although he would have preferred not to because of the heat, custom forced him to wear a coat and tie whenever he preached in Manaus. He left his coat and tie behind, however, when traveling into the interior.

Richard was glad to be able to leave the river ministry in the hands of young Pastor Filemon, who had accompanied him on the last trip. Almir Alves Ribeiro would serve as pastor of the Second Baptist Church in Manaus while he was in the States.

Later, in a letter to the Cherokee Baptist Church of Memphis, Tennessee, where the Walkers would spend most of their furlough, Richard wrote about his last two years in Manaus:

> These last two years in Manaus and on the Amazon River are now two years of testimony to the faithfulness of God. First of all, He was faithful to His word. Seldom was the Good News proclaimed when no one gladly embraced it. If you could have been with us at San Pedro where Julião gathered his family and friends to hear God's Word read and explained, you could have seen God draw into His kingdom Julião's entire family and some of his neighbors; or perhaps at the little island of Trinidade where 36 were saved in one night of preaching (two sermons of about one hour each) or at Paricá or Catuá or Copeá or a hundred other places where God was faithful in saving over 500 adults.

Chapter 7

Their tour of three arduous but rewarding years in Brazil finished, the Walkers returned to the United States on July 1, 1967, their twelfth wedding anniversary. Through the generosity of Cherokee Baptist Church of Memphis, Tennessee, they were furnished a missionary furlough house. This would be their home base from the first of September until they sailed on June 17, 1968, to begin their second term of service in Brazil.

While on furlough, the Walkers traveled extensively in bringing their missionary story to as many persons as possible. Such contacts would prove valuable in acquiring friends who would later contribute to meet needs on the mission field in Amazonas. Also, it would help even more in later years when the Walkers needed volunteer missionaries to go to Brazil for two-week periods.

Cherokee Baptist Church itself donated a tape recorder and Tupperware. It also furnished medicine and supplies that the missionaries took back with them.

They returned to Brazil with renewed zeal for the work they had left, as Richard again became pastor of the Second Baptist Church at Manaus and resumed his river ministry. The church not only had the two congregations at Catuá and Copeá, but also the work at Terra Nova in the interior, the ministry in Gloria congregation in Manaus, and the congregation of Coaban de Flores, also in Manaus.

In their first newsletter after their return to the field, they sent Christmas greetings for 1968:

> No warm fire and hot chocolate, but a fan and iced tea; no smell of cedar and tinsel but the refreshing smell of approaching rain and the continual bearing of fruits and blooming of flowers. It's Christmas! But the "feeling" of Christmas comes not from outward circumstances but from an inward relationship to the Christ child.
>
> Yes! We'll have a tree and presents. We'll decorate our home and

display our cards. But without those other nostalgic surroundings, it's not outwardly the same. Christmas is seeing God work in strange and wonderful ways through all eternity.

The first year after their return was indeed a busy one. Richard preached 222 regular sermons, 32 special sermons, made eight trips up river, saw 150 accept Christ and baptized 32, in addition to conducting a funeral and a wedding. He also preached two sermons a week and held prayer meetings when in Manaus.

In January 1969, he also became pastor of the Ebenezer Baptist Church in Manaus. He continued as Secretary of Evangelism for the Amazonas Baptist Convention.

Serving as host pastor for the annual state convention in February 1969 proved to be no small task, especially since he was elected as president of the state Pastors' Conference, elected to serve on the State Board and also to serve on the board of the Ida Nelson Baptist School. In May he assumed the duties of substitute state Executive Secretary, to serve for one year while Lonnie Doyle was on furlough.

Richard had already been elected in August 1968 as president of the Amazon English School Board and was reelected in May 1969. In addition to all that, he oversaw the construction of a chapel at Coaban de Flores in Manaus. As always, Bea continued to serve alongside her husband, always supporting him while at the same time staying tremendously busy with her own responsibilities of the home and the local church.

Richard's first trip upriver after his return from furlough was plagued by difficulties. His departure was delayed five days because his equipment from the States was held up in customs. He had to head for home three days early because the boat sprang a leak on the way to Catuá. He and the boat boy crawled over the bottom of the hull in a vain effort to find the leak, so they decided it must be under the motor. This damage would necessitate pulling the boat out of the water to repair it, something they were not yet ready to do. That night they had to take water out of the boat several times.

The Sunday morning service was scheduled to begin at 9:00 A.M. and a discouraged and dejected Richard felt he must start back home before the boat got so bad he would have to have it pulled out of the water. The riverbank was muddy and so was he. The boat was leaking. It was raining. But as he approached the service, he heard the people singing a song that told the story of a person who gets to the judgment and finds all he can say is "But they didn't tell me about this Christ." With a restored sense of purpose, he went into the service much happier.

Richard stopped in Coari to take on diesel fuel, then the crew had to bail out water eight times during the thirty hours it took to get to Manaus. Even though he took another trip upriver from September 27 to October 3, it was not until January 1963 that the boat was recaulked.

The Walkers were saddened when their colleague Ona Belle Cox, who had headed the Manaus missionary school attended by Winston and Boyd, died at age forty-nine on April 19, 1969, in St. Louis, Missouri. A special memorial service was held in the Second Baptist Church.

In 1969 Southern Baptists launched an aggressive program of evangelism called "Campaign of the Americas." In June, Richard wrote that this meant for most in the United States large gatherings in big churches, a week's meeting in the home church, or the opportunity for the pastor to preach in a different church.

His idea of a Brazilian-style campaign was vastly different, as he wrote:

> So let's take the Gospel to the Amazon River in Brazil. We are just going 500 miles but you will feel every mile of the entire trip. There are no planes and no roads for cars, but a tremendous river-road carved by the finger of God in ages past. It does not waste away but grows larger and more beautiful with the passing years.
>
> We travel about eight miles an hour; that way you can enjoy the scenery. Also, the boat won't go any faster. This is our transportation. At times you might have a few extra passengers who will have much less trouble going downstream if you will give them a pull upstream.
>
> We will travel at night also in order to conserve time. Outside of the motor getting hot, the water pump giving trouble and the spotlight going out, we will have little trouble. It's 9:00 A.M. March 26, 1969. Deadline: 9:00 A.M. March 30—500 miles up river.
>
> We arrive and find things in good order. We find no church building, for there is no church out here. But, if a group of God's people (some baptized and some not) gathered together for worship and evangelization is a church, then we have one here too. Here is where

we will meet one time. It is a home typical of all homes in this great Amazon area.

This home is located some six miles inland from the big river. The mother, father and three grown daughters accepted Christ the last time we were here. This is Lake Catuá. Most all of your preaching will be in homes like this one. Most of your crowds will be relatively small and a large percentage of them will be kin to one another. You know that when one accepts Christ it will make it easier for the others, and if someone verbally says no first, it will be very hard for others to make an affirmative decision at that time. And so you pray hard and preach simple.

But how would you preach to a group of people, a large portion of whom had never heard the Gospel? Oh, they know who Jesus is, but they do not personally KNOW JESUS. You give an invitation that stresses TRUST but also COMPLETE SURRENDER. In this group eleven adults accepted Christ as their personal Savior. This happens time and time again. On this particular trip we have the joy of seeing 42 people trust Jesus as their Savior.

You will be privileged to preach in eight different homes like this in addition to visiting in others and witnessing personally to other families. Some of them, too, will accept Christ as you talk to them about His Salvation. . . .

. . . A white shirt, tie, and suit would hardly go well in such circumstances as these. So, you fit in. This calls for sports shirt, khaki pants and boots for me. The boots are for protection from the many insects that will attack you. Each of these will draw blood if you don't get to him in time. God has been very gracious; I have never been sick on one of these trips.

Of course, "fittin' in" means eating things you wouldn't ordinarily eat. It won't hurt you; you just don't like it. It also means talking their language. . . .

. . . For a rest now and then from the strain of preaching and visiting, you will get to fish a bit. You don't have to be a first-class fisherman to catch a fish here. I am sending a picture of a 22-pound catfish. . . . I don't think I would swap the privilege of fishing for an air-conditioned automobile. Bea may beg to differ with me here, but she has never caught a 22-pound catfish!

Back home 13 days later. You have traveled five and preached eight days and always to lost people. God has given a harvest and yet it is not enough. The rate of winning must increase sharply.

This was one of four trips to the interior that he would make during his second year after returning from furlough. His second year had started off fast when he was reelected to the Executive Committee at the annual mission meeting at Forteleza in 1969. He also was named to the Finance Committee of the Mission, as well as chairman of the Evangelism and Church Development Committee, and chosen to serve on the Aviation Committee.

Meanwhile, Bea was elected as the Mission Statistician, and on July 2, 1969, the couple received their five-year service pins from the Foreign Mission Board. Richard did extensive remodeling of the old Eric Nelson home so that it could serve as the offices for the Amazonas Baptist Convention.

With funds provided from friends in the United States, headed by the Rev. Al Cullum, Richard was able to supervise the building of the *Eurico Nelson II* launch. In addition, he supervised the remodeling of the educational annex of the Second Baptist Church. All of this forced him to resign as pastor of the Ebenezer Church of Manaus after only one year.

The last week in May was an exciting one for him since he would take the *Eurico Nelson II* on its maiden voyage. It was built with a $9,000 gift from friends and churches. The new boat was equipped with a 101-horsepower Detroit diesel two-cycle marine engine, one spotlight, two docking lights, two navigation lights, two twelve-volt batteries, and a twenty-two-inch propeller.

The 45-foot-long, 11-foot-wide vessel could make fifteen miles per hour. It had two double bunks sleeping four, with several hammock hooks and benches to sit on. It contained two 110-gallon fuel tanks and an 80-gallon water tank with a shower, kitchen, and marine head.

At 7:00 A.M. on May 21, 1970, the *Eurico Nelson II* was off on its first trip. Even though there was a good moon the night before, Richard chose to travel mostly by day so they could both see and hear the new boat perform. Going upriver, they stayed close to the bank to avoid the strong current.

He took the wheel at 6:00 P.M. in order to be the first to use the new lights. Shortly after 8:00 P.M., he saw some grass and weeds in front of him. He was about to turn out when he saw a 20-foot log extending into the river. Knowing that the log would damage the boat severely, he cut the motor and glided into what he thought would be a bunch of grass and trash. It turned out to be a point of land jutting into the river.

The boat, however, was undamaged as it glided onto the strip of land, with half of the boat on land and half of it in the water. After only thirteen hours, he had run the *Eurico Nelson II* aground on its maiden voyage! He and the boat boy vainly tried to dislodge it with the 3-by-12 gangplank board. A man advised them that a boat from a farm down the river would be by in the morning with twenty men aboard.

When the men came by at 7:00 A.M. they teased Richard about his running the boat aground, but put their shoulders to the bow and pushed the boat back into the water in fifteen minutes. He decided to dock at the house of the man who had offered advice and was now there to help them. He invited the man, his wife, and their three children to come on board the boat for a service. After he preached and gave an invitation, the couple and two of their children accepted Christ as their Savior.

When they arrived at Iauara, not a village but merely a place along the river, Richard was pleased to find that the new church building was almost completed. He held services in the floating home of the pastor, with three decisions made for Christ.

Turning off the Amazon, they went up the Purus River and then along a creek called Berury. When Richard used the new generator—made possible by Lottie Moon mission offerings—to turn on an electric light, a small boy who had never seen electric lights before became terrified. When the lad got over the scare, he couldn't quit talking about it.

The *Eurico Nelson II* had performed beyond expectations on the eight-day trip. It was the first time that Richard had not had some trouble with the motor or boat.

Soon after the maiden voyage of the new boat, he took his family with him on a seven-day trip during which he preached twice, with three decisions and four baptisms resulting. When Bea had stayed behind, she had taken care of all the preparations for his trips. This time, they went off and left behind in their refrigerator all of the meat purchased for the trip. They relied on the usual Spam and Vienna sausage, and fish that they caught on the trip.

Meanwhile, Winston was developing considerable skills as an artist. A reproduction of his oil painting of his father appeared in the December 1970 issue of *The Commission,* a missionary publication of the Southern Baptist Convention, and again in January, 1971, in the newsletter of the Cherokee Baptist Church of Memphis, Tennessee.

Richard found that even though God had raised up others to continue the river ministry of pioneer Eric Nelson, and even though these followers had traveled many miles of the Amazon, rarely did they find places not previously visited by Nelson. An example of the far-reaching effects of Nelson's efforts was shown when three women joined the Second Baptist Church at Manaus. When Richard visited their father, he found that he had been converted under the preaching of Nelson at Teresina, a thousand miles down river and a thousand miles inland.

One of these who was carrying on the work of Nelson was 82-year-old Herculano Oliveira, to whom Richard paid tribute in a June 1971 article in *The Commission.* In addition to his few household belongings, Herculano had only a canoe and one paddle. For many years he had walked beside Nelson, the "Apostle of the Amazon." When Nelson died in 1939, Herculano continued to carry the message of good tidings up and down the Amazon and her tributaries.

"I always ask God to give me two fish each day as I travel preaching His Word—one to eat and one to trade for farinha," Herculano said. "In all these years, God has never failed to give me two fish each day."

One frustration Herculano felt was in not being sure just where God wanted him to stop to preach. There are 40,000 miles of navigable rivers, so Herculano could never be sure. So he prayed: "Lord, as I paddle down the river, if you have someone to whom I must go with your saving word, let it rain just as I am passing their house."

Herculano declared, "Many times an entire family has accepted Christ when God has led me by His rain."

Richard noted that even as Nelson had been expendable, Herculano would soon be expendable but that God would call up new missionaries to carry on the work.

Winston and Boyd had always attended Brazilian schools. During the first two years after their return to Brazil, however, the Walkers, along with four other missionary families, had hired a teacher to come to Manaus to teach their children. Classes ranged from the first through the eighth grade, but did not include high school.

When Winston reached the ninth grade, the Walkers had to make the difficult decision to send their fourteen-year-old fifty miles down river to the New Tribes Mission School at Puraquequara. It was one of the most painful decisions they had ever made.

The mission school was a puritanical one, with few conveniences. He took his baths in the Amazon and ate such exotic foods as lizards and alligators. A generator provided two hours of electricity daily for study purposes, but he could not be reached by telephone. He was able to go home once a month for an overnight trip.

Bea had spent a productive three years after their return to Manaus. In addition to teaching Winston and Boyd four hours a day, she had served two years as Mission Statistician. She also had prepared meals and had acted as hostess for 418 registered guests in their home, some staying for only a meal but others for up to two weeks. Her parents visited for two weeks, but most of their guests were Brazilians, many of them native pastors from the interior.

Bea could tell when they planned a prolonged visit if they brought their hammocks. If they planned to stay only overnight, they would sleep in a regular bed. The mission house had plenty of hooks on which to hang hammocks. She found that keeping "the home fires burning" while missionary Richard traveled the rivers was an ongoing challenge. When someone asked her what she did while he was gone, she quipped, "I cry a lot!"

The return of the Lonnie Doyles from furlough had relieved Richard from some of his administrative duties during his third year, but he still continued serving on many committees and was elected as vice-president of the Amazonas State Convention. The construction of the sanctuary of Second Baptist Church was completed, with an illuminated cross beautifying the front of the church. The illuminated cross was a first among Baptist churches in Amazonas and brought both compliments and criticism.

A total of thirteen trips were made upriver during the third year, with a total of 560 running hours on the *Eurico Nelson II*. He had also conducted six evangelism clinics as part of his job as state evangelism secretary.

Now in April 1971, their thoughts were beginning to turn to the year of furlough in the United States. They would arrive home on May 31. The First Baptist Church of Paducah, Kentucky, was providing a beautifully furnished home and a car for them to drive. The Walkers, however, would have an extensive schedule that would have them bringing their missionary story to many places. Although they eagerly looked forward to reuniting with family and friends, they also were eager to expand their circle of friends.

Their travels would take them on many trips, including Glorieta Baptist Assembly near Santa Fe, New Mexico, where their work was highlighted with a slide presentation and dialogue between officials and the Walkers. A Foreign Mission Board photographer had visited the Walkers just before their furlough and had taken many photos of them at work. Based on this extensive coverage, their work was featured in the February 1972 issue of *The Commission* magazine. The magazine for *Mission Friends* also carried pictures and script of the maiden voyage of the *Eurico Nelson II*.

Chapter 8

Once again the Walkers were back in the United States on a well-deserved furlough, this time in the Blue Grass State of Kentucky. It had been a particularly gruelling second term in Brazil because of the many tasks added to their regular duties.

They were hardly settled into their Paducah home before they were off to North Kingston, Rhode Island, for speaking engagements on July 4 at Green Meadows Baptist Church. Not only did Richard preach at the services, but the two showed artifacts from Amazonas, with full explanations, and discussed needs in the mission field. Among other speaking engagements, Bea addressed the adult Sunday School assembly while there.

From then on, the Walkers fulfilled many preaching and speaking engagements in churches, youth camps, and church groups in several states. He spoke to the high school football squad of Benton, Arkansas, on September 17. He was the speaker for pastors' conferences in several states. And naturally, both spoke at many Paducah area churches.

Richard returned to his alma mater, speaking twice on February 20, 1972, at the College of the School of the Ozarks. Besides being asked to speak, he was awarded the Distinguished Alumni Award of the school, located at Point Lookout, Missouri. The Walkers also returned to Cherokee Baptist Church, where they had furloughed in 1968–69, for several speaking engagements. Richard ended the furlough year by speaking eleven times during the period from July 23–August 20 to the First Baptist Church in Paducah.

In addition to honorariums for speaking, they received numerous gifts for the Amazonas mission field. The largest of these was $6,000 from the First Baptist Church of Waurika, Oklahoma, for a new boat motor, including shipping and installation costs. The First Baptist Church of Paducah contributed $2,070 for chapels.

As they prepared to return to Brazil, they began to feel that it was not right and that God was telling them not to return—not then. After much soul-searching, they made their decision not to return to their beloved adopted land, not understanding why. They would SEND all monies and other gifts to the Amazonas field; they would not be TAKING them.

Late that night on the day that they had made this decision, Stanford Andrus, chairman of the Pastor Search Committee of the First Baptist Church of Murray, Kentucky, called and rather apologetically said, "We have followed you all over western Kentucky, and since you are a foreign missionary, we don't know why, but we feel that God has called us to ask you to come and talk to us about the possibilities." Unknown to Richard, the committee members had sat in on several occasions when he had preached to totally new congregations.

The committee met with him several times, then asked him to preach a trial sermon before the church congregation. When the church voted the following Sunday on issuing a call, there were only 5 no votes, with more than 450 voting affirmatively. As a result, the Walkers began their ministry as pastor and wife in August 1972. It was quite fitting that this church should be the one to extend the call since it had supplied the funds for Eric Nelson's construction in 1918 of the *Buffalo,* the boat he had used for his river ministry. A beautiful red brick church just off the county seat square, First Baptist, along with Murray State University, was the hub of activity for the entire area.

The ministry at Murray proved quite successful as the church experienced revival in every area. Baptisms increased dramatically and the ministry to the students at Murray State was revived. Contributions almost tripled and Sunday School attendance grew from 500 to 750. The church acquired additional space by purchasing and remodeling a supermarket adjoining its property.

Most importantly, during their three-year stay in Murray, God called into full-time Christian service some thirty-six young adults, most of whom are now serving in some capacity at home or on the foreign mission field. Richard was active in associational and state committees, as well as in the local church leadership.

Rather suddenly, however, he and Bea began to feel God's call that it was time for them to return once again to the Amazon. Winston had finished high school and had a job, so he would be unable to return with them.

They realized that it would be a severe test for them to leave him behind and take sixteen-year-old Boyd back with them. They wondered how they could break the news to Boyd as they sought God's help through prayer. One day he came home from school and came into the room where his parents were.

"You know, I sat there today and all I could think about was Brazil," he blurted out. They soon were assured that he, too, wanted to return to Brazil.

The Foreign Mission Board reappointed them without question. Again, they would return to Manaus and to the river ministry. The only difference would be that they would live in a different house.

God would use those three years in Murray to form a strong base for volunteer missions support in the future. In fact, Owen Billington and Dan Shipley of Murray would be on the original Board of Directors of the future Amazon Mission Organization.

Chapter 9

In 1975 the Walkers plunged back into the work at Manaus, and Richard soon resumed the boat trips up river. Their work would be aided by an offset press and a large camera to make negatives for the offset. These were donated by the First Baptist Church of Paducah, Kentucky, and would be used by Lonnie Doyle in his work.

The first two trips would be short ones in August 1975. Richard, accompanied by Boyd and missionary Wayne Pringle, preached at Paracuúba and at a preaching point at Olaria, then returned home the same day. They arranged to go back later for a baptism and celebration of the Lord's supper.

Just how much concern and solicitude Richard had for the people of his river ministry is shown by the fact that he recorded in detail an account in his diary of a man released from a tuberculosis sanitarium as cured only to become paralyzed after bathing in the river while he was quite hot. The man, who lay in his hammock, wanted to be baptized and Richard prayed fervently that he could be when they returned.

Richard, Boyd, and missionary kid Danny Partin returned to Paracuúba two weeks later on August 23. Richard preached, then baptized five persons, including the paralyzed man. Meanwhile, he had sent a canoe to Manaus to pick up missionary Glenn Grober, who arrived in time to preach before the Lord's supper was served. They stayed overnight and Glenn preached in the Sunday morning service.

The group broke its routine by eating at an exotic restaurant on the lake before Glenn again preached to a sizable crowd at Olaria. They returned to Manaus that night.

Richard, Boyd, and Amazi, the boat boy, took their first prolonged river trip, an eight-day journey to Berury and mostly on the lake area near Iauara. Because of a late start from Manaus, Richard had to pull into shore after only two hours due to darkness. He took advantage of the opportunity to preach to a crowd who had gathered at a floating store.

Since none of the group had a Bible or had ever heard the story of creation, he began by telling them about the Old and New Testament and the story of creation as recorded in Genesis. The crowd grew and when he asked for decisions, four men and a twenty-year-old woman accepted Christ as their Savior.

The crew had tied the boat to a tree away from the bank. Their peaceful sleep was interrupted when they discovered that large ants living in the tree had filled the boat.

Stopping by the floating house of their long-time friend, José Carvalho, they found that he had been ill twice with malaria during the past two years. He said he had gotten it in Lake Piorini, exactly where Richard planned to open new work. José promised to get some slabs of saboeirana, a handsome dark wood, for the Walkers to make a table for their living room.

Another old friend who was overjoyed to see Richard again was Herculano, now 86. His 49-year-old son Isaias directed the mission work in the area of the large lake, but needed a motor for his boat. With eleven children and few resources, he could not afford to buy one. Richard hoped to be able to help him soon.

He set up a service within the lake despite being bitten by a beetle the night before. He had squashed the beetle under his arm while he slept, then had unknowingly spread the secretions over his chest and face. This caused what appeared to be deep burns. The bite caused considerable burning, but he decided not to abandon the trip.

A smaller aluminum boat called the jon boat was now being used because it contained a Johnson-powered motor. It could travel where the larger launch could not and came in handy to bring people to the baptism.

On one occasion, Richard preached to an extremely noisy crowd of about seventy-five persons and was surprised that three of them made decisions to accept Christ as their Savior. On the very next occasion, he preached on "Hell" to what he described as his quietest and most attentive audience. This time five made decisions.

Richard managed to get in plenty of successful fishing on this trip despite preaching nine times, with fourteen decisions and thirteen baptisms.

He would make three more extended and four short river trips in 1975, with Boyd accompanying him on one long trip and two of the short ones. Each trip offered new excitement and different possibilities as his zeal to convert the people of Amazonas never seemed to flag.

The Walkers had to make the difficult choice on October 11 of turning down an invitation to a fellowship luncheon from their dearest friends, Moacyr and Eunice Alves, so that Richard could keep an appointment to preach at the home of a believer in a little village called Iranduba. The Alveses' impressive guest list included the president of the Brazilian Baptist Convention, an army general, the most prominent evangelistic singer in Brazil, and a prominent Manaus lawyer who was also the brother of the governor of the state of Amazonas.

When he was drenched by boisterous waves as he tried to cross the Amazon, Richard thought of the comfortable fellowship and delicious meal he had turned down. Before he reached midriver, however, the waters suddenly became smooth, without so much as a ripple of a wave. Furthermore, seven persons made decisions after he had preached the Gospel. He made the perilous trip by night back over the usually rough but now smooth waters of the Amazon.

On a trip later in October, he planned to tow the older version of the *Eurico Nelson* boat for use in the work at Lake Berury, but it began to leak badly. He tried to use the pump from the new launch, but it wouldn't work. He and Boyd resorted to dipping water out, but managed to get the boat only as far as Paracuúba. They decided it would be best not to risk dragging it any farther, so they donated it to the congregation there. Richard bemoaned the fact that four years ago he could have sold the boat for $2,500, but had thought that amount too little.

On this trip, they found that José de Calvalho had been ill again with malaria and had not been able to get the wood that Richard had requested for a table. They shared some farinha with him and José gave them a matrishão fish.

The next day Boyd almost severed his father's forefinger when, not knowing that Richard was behind him, he closed the door on the boat. Richard went to a small hospital where mercurochrome and bandages were applied, then he decided to continue the trip since it would be too late to stitch the finger by the time he got back to Manaus.

For more than six years, he had wanted to start work in Lake Piorini. Now he was even more eager when he found out that there had been no evangelical work there. He found a man who wanted a ride into the lake, so Richard finally had his chance. It took ten and a half hours to reach the man's house, which was still outside Lake Piorini. The man's father was blind from cataracts and his sister was mute, but could hear.

After Richard conducted a worship service in the old man's house, four persons made decisions for Christ. Despite being pestered by swarms of mosquitoes, eleven persons accepted Christ as Savior in a night service in the schoolhouse. Boyd, who suffered from mosquito bites more than Richard, thought it would be better to hold the next service in the daytime.

They entered Lake Piorini for the first time the next morning and found three houses close together. The people told them that no one had ever told them of the Gospel, so they arranged to hold a service. Boyd went out along the lake, which was eight to ten miles wide, in the jon boat and brought in a boatload of people. Nine persons made decisions after the service, then Richard talked to a woman in a hammock who had given birth that morning. She, too, accepted Christ.

That afternoon the crew decided to fish as a storm raged some distance from them. When they started to leave, Boyd wanted to turn back because he thought he had seen a big snake along the water's edge, while Richard thought it was a dead pirarucú, a very large fish. Boyd was right, so they returned to the boat for a rifle and Amazi, the boat boy.

The trio went ashore a bit above where the snake was peacefully digesting his dinner. Its head was to their right and eight to twelve inches under water. From the vantage point of a nearby tree limb, each shot one time at the snake's head, but the effects of the .22 caliber bullets were practically nil after traveling through eight inches of water.

Devising another plan of action, they tied a one-fourth inch nylon rope to its tail since approximately six feet of the snake was out of water. They then cut away all limbs and brush so they would not be hindered in pulling the snake into the lake.

As they began to pull the anaconda into the lake, it began to twist and turn vigorously. They waited until his contractions caused it to regurgitate the five-and-a-half-foot alligator it had swallowed. Then they headed for shore as fast as the little outboard would take them. Boyd ran the bow of the boat onto the sandy beach as Richard jumped out and ran up the bank, dragging the snake behind him. He did not know what their task would be when they turned around, but it proved to be uneventful.

The snake lay there and squirmed some. Richard learned later that when you pull a snake through the sand by his tail, the sand gets under his scales and immobilizes him. All the fight was gone out of him as Richard shot him through the head. The local people skinned the snake for them. Later, when they returned to the place, they found the snake skin laid out and it measured 13 feet, 10-1/2 inches and was 20 inches around at its widest. Richard remarked that before it was measured, he was sure that it was 30 feet long! Richard also insists that Boyd's version of the encounter would be different and much more exciting.

That night they held a service in the house of a man who had long wanted one. A crowd of twenty-five to thirty persons gathered and there were ten decisions. Still farther into the lake the next day at the village of Liberdade, seven responded to the Gospel. On reaching Liberdade, they had taken a five-hour journey or approximately seventy-five miles, along the lake.

From there the missionaries crossed the lake that afternoon to a place on a creek. The man of the house said it would be difficult to have a service because the workers, when they came in from cutting jute, had to go out to kill something for supper. At the place where they were to hold services that night, the man of the house did not come in until 8 p.m., then said he had to catch a fish for supper.

The man was fishing with a spear, so he and Boyd fished for a half hour without success. Since the family would have no fish for supper, Richard gave them three fish from the boat's refrigerator.

By this time it was 9:00 P.M., so Richard announced that it was too late to have a service. One of the men said surely not since he had come for that purpose. Richard reconsidered, preached to them from

1 Peter 1: 1–3, and led them in singing choruses. Six persons made decisions for Christ. Richard reflected on how God had reopened the service that he had tried to close.

Not only was he a good fisherman of men on this trip but he proved his adeptness at the sport of fishing. He had already caught some fish with his net, but now his net caught one weighing 35 and 1/2 pounds. No more estimating the weight of these fish—scales were brought and accurate weights made.

This did not detract from his main mission of witnessing for Christ, and he took advantage of every opportunity. Seeing some men standing on a bank, he felt compelled to stop to witness to them. Even though he pleaded with them that they not make a decision unless they really meant it, six accepted Christ.

By this time, Richard's finger looked bad, but he had decided that it would stay on. Also, the bushing in the boat was giving trouble. Amazi, the boat boy, managed to repair it temporarily, while Richard used the opportunity to visit with the folks of a little village. A man reluctantly agreed to have a service and four responded to the Gospel.

Richard recorded his thoughts as he left Lake Piorini:

> I had been in the lake for four days. There had been forty plus professions of faith in Christ, all adults. I was at the wheel of the boat and thinking about those who had found their Savior. As I contemplated the situation I was saying, almost out loud, "Lord, these new Christians have no one to teach them; no deacon, no pastor, no Sunday School teacher. In fact, no one has been a Christian more than four days. All they have are the Bibles I left with them and the Holy Spirit in their hearts."
>
> At that point, it seemed as if God reached down and slapped my face and said, "Little missionary, what more do you think they need besides your prayers?"
>
> That encounter with God changed my missionary strategy from dependence on man and what we could do to keep these people from drifting back into their old way of life to dependence on God. From this point on, prayer ceased to be a means to bolster our missionary work and became the major responsibility of our missionary work.

Moving slowly through stumps in a small branch of the Amazon, they got to a larger branch and then arrived at Coari at noon. Here they would buy fuel and have someone make them a new bushing for the boat. Richard preached to a crowd of a hundred persons at the Wednesday night prayer service at the Baptist church in Coari.

Having been gone for eight days and having turned sixteen on the trip without the benefit of cake or candles, Boyd was eager to get home. Amazi was also homesick for his wife and two-and-a-half-year-old daughter. Richard, too, wanted to get home, but he felt that there was still work they needed to do first.

They traveled on to Catuá to the home of Raimundo, one of his first converts when he began the river ministry more than ten years ago. That night he decided to try his luck at fishing. He took a large hook, tied a four-pound weight on it along with a whole fish, and dropped it into the water. The next morning he found that he had caught a sixty-pound catfish. He strained his back pulling it up to weigh it. He gave the fish to the people there.

Richard decided to go into Lake Ipixuma, but had to go in the jon boat while leaving Amazi out in the river with the launch because the water was so low in the lake. He made some forty visits in the homes before preaching to the congregation there. Six persons made decisions.

The next day he found that he needed the wisdom of Solomon as he was called upon to make a difficult decision. The town drunk wanted him to help solve his problem. He had been married to a woman by a priest, which is not a legal marriage in Brazil.

They had one child, but the woman had left him because of his drinking. Presently, he was living with another woman and they had two children. Now he wanted to straighten out his life and wondered whether he should go back to the first woman or stay with the second.

Richard told him he would have to think about that for a while. In the meantime, he talked to the father of the first woman and he told Richard that his daughter would never go back to the man. The missionary returned to the couple, counseled with them to take what they had, dedicated it to the Lord, and let Him forgive them of their sins.

They both accepted Christ as their Savior and wanted to be

baptized. Under the rules of the Brazilian Baptist Convention, however, they would have to be legally married before being baptized.

After fourteen days of what Richard termed as a "glorious trip," they arrived in Manaus on Wednesday, October 29. He had preached twenty-four times, with eighty-four decisions and two baptisms.

Richard, along with Amazi and his wife, Maria, and two-and-a-half-year-old daughter, Francinete, took one more prolonged river trip in 1975. They left Manaus at 10:30 A.M. on Thursday, December 4. The trip would be longer because the water was low, preventing the possibilities of shortcuts. They passed Manacapurú at 7:00 P.M. and docked at the mouth of Manacapurú Lake.

While visiting in the home of one of the members of the church at Iaura, Richard finally was presented with a slab of saboeirana wood, which he desired for a table. This member had a daughter who would be fifteen years old on January 1. The fifteenth birthday is a big occasion for a Brazilian girl, as it represents her debut into society and womanhood. The parents were postponing the party until January 15 so that they could barbecue a beef. Some five hundred persons were expected to attend the feast.

That Saturday night at Codajás Richard preached to an overflow crowd of two hundred persons. The missionaries would not leave there until Wednesday night as they employed the jon boat to visit the people around the area and in Lake Miuá.

Richard visited in the home of Francisco, a leper who had become a believer five years ago. The leper's joy at seeing his friend made Richard ashamed that he had not visited him sooner. Francisco said he had felt an unexplained joy for five days, and now he knew his joy had been because his missionary was coming. While Richard remained to preach at Francisco's home, he sent word back to the pastor at Codajás to preach at the service there in Richard's place. Seven persons responded when Richard extended an invitation.

At the request of Francisco's mother, he visited her daughter and son at home. Here he found a scene of misery as all of this family, with the exception of Francisco's mother and one daughter, were lepers. He found the daughter, who had been bitten by a poisonous snake six months earlier, in a hammock and too weak to arise. He did not give her longer than six months to live.

Her twenty-five-year-old brother was badly deformed from

leprosy. Another brother had died at age twenty only a year before. None of the family attended church services because the people would leave if they did. Despite all of this, Francisco presented Richard with his fattest hen and five eggs for a love offering.

In addition to preaching and baptizing at points on the way back, Richard helped a group at Lake Berury to organize a mission separate from the church in the village of Berury. He left them with the responsibility of finding a church site and cutting the lumber to start construction. During the eleven-day trip, he had preached fourteen times, with eighteen decisions and six baptisms.

Richard made one more trip in 1975, a daytime trip on December 20 to Paracuúba in the jon boat. Although he got home before dark, he received a soaking because of the rough water in front of Manaus and down river a ways.

Chapter 10

Little did the Walkers know when they began 1976 that this would be their final full year in Manaus. Richard wasted no time in getting the new year under way as he and Boyd set off on a one-day trip on January 3.

Traveling in the jon boat, the smaller aluminum vessel, thirty-five miles from Manaus to Lake Iranduba on the Solimões River, the two arrived in a heavy rain. They stopped at the house of Solon, who told them that because of the rain no one else would show up for services. They persuaded Solon to wait until the rain had passed. Three more families did arrive and after Richard had preached, four made first-time decisions.

After going farther into the lake, Boyd and Raias Batista Salgado, a young native preacher who would serve in the river ministry for about a year, went out and invited the people. Richard preached to twenty-three persons, with ten decisions. The missionaries were able to get back to Manaus by 6:00 P.M. that same day.

Accompanying Richard and Boyd on their trip to Iauara and Berury on January 9–16 were Dr. Moacyr Alves, Raias Batista Salgado, and Amazi, the boat boy. Moacyr was now president of the Amazonas Baptist Convention and attorney general for the state of Amazonas.

The trip proved to be an eventful one. At Iauara, José de Cavalho killed a steer for the church in celebration of his daughter's fifteenth birthday. People came in canoes and in boats 25 to 50 feet in length until a crowd of nearly five hundred jammed even the middle aisle and sides of the church, then overflowed to the outside. Richard, however, realized more than ever the importance of house-to-house ministry when only seven of the huge crowd made decisions for Christ.

Accompanying the crew to Berury was eight-six-year-old Herculano. A group on the lake wanted to organize a mission separate from the one in the town of Berury. At a business meeting, Raias was elected as pastor with a salary of about seventy dollars a month. Part of the money would be supplied by the Amazonas Baptist Convention.

Richard knew that this would be his last time to visit and fellowship with his dear friend Herculano, who had served his Lord well for so many years. He was now very frail and eighty-six years old. With the missionary's imminent return to the United States, this great servant of God would go to his reward long before the Walkers would return to Brazil.

When the boat docked in the mouth of Lake Cuiuana, Richard was approached by a twenty-year-old woman who had been ranting for three days. The group prayed for her in her home and asked God to give her a good night's rest. She, as well as a drunk who had been following the missionaries around, attended the service that night. Neither disturbed the service, however, and among three who made decisions for Christ was the drunk.

During the eight-day trip, Richard preached six times, with eighteen decisions and eight baptisms.

Thurmon Bryant, missionary to São Paulo, made a record of the trip as he and his son David accompanied Richard and Amazi on a one-day trip on January 2. Along also were Tom and Libby Robuck, new missionaries to Brazil. David was thrilled by being allowed to steer the *Eurico Nelson II* for a considerable time.

The group arrived at the Baptist congregation at Paracuúba at 9:30 A.M. in the midst of Sunday School, but received warm handshakes and embraces, then the Sunday School resumed. Youngsters entertained them by singing choruses and reciting Bible verses, with David reciprocating by reciting John 3:16 in both English and Portuguese.

Thurmon marveled how Richard and Amazi were able to find their way through the many tributaries that joined the rivers and inland lakes. He observed a man with a serious reaction to medicine that he had taken to cure a leg wound left by a sting ray. He watched as a little girl joyously welcomed her father home from Manaus. The father, in turn, gave her a half-melted popsickle, which he had carefully packed in ice for her among the fish.

Thurmon also saw an old man who could not use his Bible because he had loaned his eyeglasses to a new convert desirous of knowing more about the Scriptures. He was bemused by a father who soaped his son's hair in the back of a canoe, and by a very happy recently married couple who descended the banks of the Amazon for their bath in bathing suits. The woman then did the laundry while the man sat shaving himself with a Gillette razor. Thurmon was deeply touched when a man showed his appreciation to the missionaries for their visit by cutting two cane stalks for them to chew on as they made their way down the river.

The climax of the trip came at about 4:00 P.M. when the day was at its hottest. Richard was desirous of finding the people who had never received the Gospel, so the missionaries made their way to the island in the midst of the Solimões River. They spotted a girl who was dipping water out of the river and found out from her that there were no Christian believers in the village.

They did, however, find a Baptist who had moved into the community six months ago. He agreed to let them hold a service in his little store. They scattered to tell the people that a service would be held within half an hour. Richard preached to a small group, with seven making decisions for Christ.

Bea, along with a friend, Clarice Batista Salgado, accompanied Richard, Boyd, and Amazi on the next trip on February 1. With only scant directions to follow, they tried to find a man who had requested worship services. When they were unable to find him, they docked at the floating store of a man named Joaquim, who agreed to let them hold a service there. He continued to sell products during the service and his wife weighed up smelly half-dried meat only two feet from where Bea sat, but the attention of the crowd was good.

The law of the jungle prevailed on this trip. Traveling around the bend of a narrow parana, they were suddenly confronted by a large barge loaded with petroleum. There was not enough room for the two to pass, so the barge plowed ahead, hitting the *Eurico Nelson II* twice, and knocking it upon the bank.

Fortunately, the launch was sturdy and undamaged, but the

nerves of its passengers were a bit frayed. Clarice had been cooking beans. The stove on which she was cooking was knocked around, but she had managed to catch the pot of beans!

On their return trip, in the same parana, a man with a lantern flagged them down late at night, apparently thinking their launch was a passenger boat. Richard cut the motor down to find out what was the matter and was talking to someone at the front of the launch. Meanwhile, a half-drunken man appeared at the back door of the launch where the sleeping quarters were and Bea was dozing in the top bunk.

She screamed out that a man was on board and ran to where Richard was. The befuddled man followed her, but more slowly than she. He said he wanted a ride to a place about thirty minutes away, so they graciously gave him a ride. Richard fed him doses of some strong coffee to sober him up, then preached to him and gave him a New Testament.

As the launch was still under repair, it had no screens for this trip. The mosquitoes swarmed in as the boat came close to the bank in the narrow paranas. The Brazilians told Bea that the mosquitoes liked to bite her because she was so white, but she wondered how insects could tell what color she was in the dark.

She observed that unlike others in the area, the people of Lake Purupurú had one or two canoes with motors at each home and had high television antennas, thus indicating that they had their own generators. Obviously, the people of this area were more affluent.

The Walkers arrived in Manaus at 11:40 P.M., but their arrival was not without excitement. As she got off the boat, Bea, who could not swim, slipped into the river. Fortunately, Richard was holding her hand and promptly pulled her out!

Richard's next trip involved a four-hour airplane flight to preach at revival services of the Baptist church at Bosque on the Rio Branco in the state of Acre. Getting off a day late because the scheduled plane did not arrive the first day, he had to find accommodations in a rather modern hotel at his own expense.

At Bosque he preached to crowds as large as 250, but he and the church's pastor also waded through three kilometers of mud up to their knees to hold services at an outpost. Despite the rain, a rather large crowd attended. He and the pastor borrowed horses for the return trip.

During this five-day mission, he managed to get in fifteen hours of study on his Doctor of Ministry degree. He had preached eight times, with thirteen decisions being made.

Boyd and Amazi accompanied Richard on February 24 under the threatening shadows of a storm and managed to reach the head of Patience Island about 6:00 P.M. Amazi went up to where Richard was piloting the boat and asked whether he didn't want to cross over to the bank of the river rather than continue up the side of the island. A light had already caught Richard's eye, leading him to believe that this was the place where God wanted them to stop.

The missionary trio found a large group of people gathered in a house where power was supplied by a small diesel engine and a generator. They were watching Batman and Robin combat crime on a TV screen.

The man of the house, Raimundo, finally came into the crowded living room. As Richard and he discussed his work of building boats and canoes, Raimundo was impressed when Richard showed him the *Eurico Nelson II*.

Richard finally told his purpose in coming, so at 8:30 P.M., Raimundo turned off the TV and announced that they could see TV every day, but it was not often that someone came to read the Bible. Richard noticed that many of the crowd were reluctant to quit watching TV and that the children refused to sing. Nevertheless, the undaunted missionary preached and five adults, including Raimundo, accepted Christ as Savior.

On this same trip, Richard was on his way to Lake Piorini when he decided to stop at a floating house where two boats were docked. He found that the men had just returned from a nearby lake with some 200 tambaque and 30 pirarucú, two of the most delicious fish in the world. He traded for ten pounds of the pirarucú filet and two 12-pound tambaque. He then waited until the men finished cleaning their fish before preaching to them. Nine adults made decisions for Christ.

Some of the same internal disputes that have split churches in the United States were encountered by Richard in his river ministry.

He had to mediate such a dispute at Catuá when he found that church members were upset because the treasurer, Chico Morais, had loaned church money to another member in an emergency. Richard talked to the disputants about the need for forgiveness.

Chico's son was running a high fever, was swollen and yellow, so Richard left the church's problems to the Lord in prayer and made arrangements to take the boy and his mother immediately to medical facilities in Coari. Chico said he would go before the church congregation on Sunday and ask for forgiveness. His son died twenty-four hours after entering the hospital.

Richard, Bea, and Boyd, along with Amazi and family, made an eleven-day trip from April 16 to 26 to Lago de Castanho, Parintins, Maués, and Itacoatiara. When he preached at the home of a former boat boy's mother, he found that only one person in the group had heard him when he preached there six years ago.

Bea kept busy as she played an important role during the trip. She had brought along flannel graph stories and a large number of pictures for the children to paint. She could tell that many of the children (from one to thirteen) had never held a crayon before. She taught them how to color within the lines.

At Urucará, a small village near Brazil Nut Lake (Lago de Castanho), Richard encountered some difficult problems concerning baptism. There were six candidates for baptism, but only five were accepted immediately. The sixth had been living with a woman for nine years but could not marry her because under Brazilian law she could not get a divorce from her first husband. In a secret vote, the church members voted for his being baptized, with, however, four voting against it. At that point, the man decided not to be baptized.

Another candidate for baptism, an old man, had sat through the discussions without a word, but then it was revealed that he was living with a woman to whom he was not married. As neither had been married before, they could get married. Richard told him that it would be necessary, as a prerequisite to baptism, for them to marry since they lived together. He then baptized the other four. He now understood why Lonnie Doyle had told the group to wait until Richard Walker arrived to baptize them!

Chapter 11

Bea Walker's parents celebrated their Golden Wedding Anniversary on May 27, 1976, so she returned to the States to help with the reception. While there, she visited Murray, Kentucky, where Winston was employed. When her physician was giving her a routine physical examination, he found a tumor in each breast and on her thyroid gland. Fortunately, all were benign and Bea was able to return to Brazil only two weeks after surgery.

After she returned to the missionary field, however, she still did not recover her health and lost a great deal of weight. All this provided a difficult experience for her, and all of their friends were advising Richard to take her back to the States.

Finally, they set a date to leave Manaus, but Bea felt she could not leave before a few things were done. First of all, Boyd must finish his correspondence work for graduation from high school at the University of Nebraska. Second, their Second Baptist Church of Manaus was to host the State Baptist Convention and they must be there. Third, Richard must complete his dissertation for his Doctor of Ministry degree before leaving. And last, they must finish the construction of the new missionary residence in Manaus.

Meanwhile, Boyd and his father carried on the river ministry and work in Manaus. Somewhat earlier, when Bea was traveling back to the States, the two took a six-day trip upriver along with Amazi and family from May 31 to June 5. When they arrived at the head of Patience Island, they found most of the homes abandoned because of high water. They did see one lamparina lit, so they tied up the boat there.

Richard and Boyd found a man and his wife, along with three teenagers and a baby, frying fish for their supper. Since they had already eaten, the Americans declined an invitation to supper, but decided to return later. When they returned, they found a neighbor and four other teenagers also present. They sang choruses, then

Richard talked to them from 1 Peter 1:3–5. Seven accepted Christ as Savior.

So many people crowded into the service held in a floating house in Iauara that one corner of the house began to sink. Richard quickly completed the service, with one decision for Christ, then advised the people to leave *gently*.

As the river was smooth and quiet on the way back to Iauara, Boyd decided to water ski. Many of the astonished natives had never seen anyone ski, so they thought he was running on the water!

In August 1976, the Walkers' beloved friend, Dr. Moacyr Alves, died of a heart attack ten days after surgery for a broken hip. Richard preached the funeral service to hundreds of people in the Second Baptist Church and by loudspeaker to those in the park. Others listened in the streets, which had been closed in the vicinity of the church. Moacyr's death was a tremendous personal loss to Richard and Bea.

On September 30, Richard set out on a nine-day trip upriver to Iauara and Lake Piorini accompanied by Boyd; friend Tom Moody of Murray, Kentucky; Amazi; and Pastor Elezeu with his wife, Maria, and son Edson. At Iauara, Tom was amused to find the women seated on one side of the church aisle and the men on the other side.

At Urucurizinho, they looked for the home of a man named Miguel, who had previously indicated he would like to have a service. They found him playing soccer that Saturday afternoon with the men of the community. He was enthusiastic about a service, so the mission team strung lights outside his house and held services at 7:30 P.M. After the service, Miguel told Richard that he had bought four acres of land and wanted to donate part of it on which to build a church. He had heard Richard preach previously.

Stopping at a floating house where some dozen men were consuming liquor, the missionaries were soon able to turn the subject to Jesus and His power to save from a life such as this. When they found out that the missionaries had evangelical musical records, one fellow wanted to go for his record player and to invite others to the service. It took him two hours to return and Richard had to be firm with the men during the delay to keep them from becoming drunk. There were twelve decisions made at the service.

On this trip they stopped by the home of Francisco the leper and found that he had come under the influence of a spiritist who had tried to cure his leprosy. Francisco had even become convinced that he did not have leprosy, but thought that someone had thrown a Voodoo-type hex on him. Richard preached about the Holy Spirit and His way of working with men.

During their nine-day trip, the group had preached ten sermons, with forty decisions being made.

Richard got more excitement than he had bargained for when he took twenty young people and adults from his church in Manaus on a one-day trip to Terra Nova. After arriving in a little more than two hours, he set the service for 7:30 P.M., then sent the young people out to walk the riverbanks and invite the people to the service.

It was becoming cloudy as the service began, but the youth were singing beautifully and Richard felt that he could finish the service before the storm fell. He thought the wind would subside soon, so he continued. As it increased in intensity and the raindrops began to spatter, he had to abandon the service.

The wind was also blowing the launch away from the bank. He herded the young people onto the launch since no house could take care of so large a crowd. Bea had on a bright yellow dress. Someone had given her five eggs in a plastic bag. The riverbank was already slick, and she slid down the bank, holding the eggs high above her head. Not an egg was broken, but she never was able to remove the red mud stain from her dress!

Amazi pulled the launch out into the river but tried to stay as close to the bank as possible so that if disaster struck, no life would be lost.

When the wind pushed the launch onto a sandbar, Richard ordered all men aboard to jump into the water and push the launch to free it. After a struggle, they succeeded. The girls became excited and began to sing, "With Christ in the boat, all will go well." After an hour, the rough water and high winds subsided somewhat.

The waters remained fierce, however, until the mission group reached the meeting of the Amazon and Solimões rivers, where the crossing is some ten miles wide. From there, it was safe to proceed to Manaus. They arrived at 10:00 P.M. with some nervous youngsters and a relieved pastor and wife.

With Bea's health showing no improvement and with the necessity of winding up their work in Manaus foremost, the Walkers did not take any more river trips. They would complete the new missionary residence and move into it, but they would stay in it for only five days.

The state convention, hosted by their church, was now history. Boyd had completed his final assignment for graduation, and Richard had finished all requirements for his degree. Then, and only then, was Bea willing to leave. When they left Brazil in March of 1977, they thought they would be back after a month. Instead, they would be gone from Brazil for seven years, and they would not return as missionaries to Manaus and the Upper Amazon region.

They soon realized upon their return to the States that they could not return to Brazil. Even Dr. Fowler, medical consultant for the Foreign Mission Board, told them they should not return. So they began to pray that God would lead them to a place where they could serve. The size of the church or its location did not matter.

They resigned from foreign mission service in May 1977. On their way back from Brazil, they had stopped in West Palm Beach, Florida, and spent a few days in the home of some friends who had visited them in Manaus. Richard was called upon to preach to a group that had broken off from a mother church in West Palm Beach and was now meeting in the cafeteria of a schoolhouse.

A few weeks went by, then the group called him to preach again. By this time, it was an organized church and was renting an old wooden airport hangar. The church voted unanimously for him to be their pastor. Since the church was only five weeks old when they arrived, they got in on the ground floor.

The ministry proved to be an exciting one of phenomenal growth among a caring congregation. Bea continued to be ill, but the congregation knew that this was the reason the Walkers had resigned as missionaries. They never made her feel guilty when she was unable to attend church or help her husband in his ministries.

Her inability to function as a pastor's wife because of constant fatigue continued to plague her for three more years. They had met an internist with whom they had exchanged social visits. Richard had tried to persuade Bea to schedule an appointment to see this physician, but she demurred, "No, I really don't want to. I have been to doctors all these years and no one has found anything wrong with me. I'm really quite tired and I just don't want to go."

In desperation, Richard pleaded, "Honey, not for you, but please do it for me."

As her husband put it that way, she made an appointment and went in. The doctor noticed that she had written as the reason for coming, "Fatigue."

He peered at her over his glasses and asked, "Has anyone ever suggested that you have a thyroid problem?"

"No, no, never."

"Well, I'm very suspicious of it," the doctor said.

After tests were run, it became evident that indeed Bea's thyroid was not functioning properly. The internist prescribed medicine and increased it after a month. Within weeks, she could tell a remarkable difference.

Once again she was able to be a pastor's wife. This was a real joy to her since theirs was a twenty-four-hour ministry in which the Walkers gave it their total effort and dedication. During the nearly seven years that they served as pastor and wife in West Palm Beach, some three dozen men and women dedicated their lives to full-time Christian service, and the church membership increased to more than nine hundred members.

Both Winston and Boyd had found employment and moved to their own apartments in West Palm Beach. The ministry to the Gold Coast Baptist Church was a real joy for the Walkers, but the church grew so fast in those nearly seven years that they could scarcely keep pace.

Once again they began to feel God's call to Brazil and the Amazon. They contacted the Foreign Mission Board in Richmond, Virginia, to see whether anyone had ever resigned twice and had then been reappointed for the third time. The board asked them to come in for a visit and they did.

As it had been more than four years since they had resigned from foreign missionary service, they had to go through all the preliminary steps, including psychiatric tests. They passed and were reappointed in October 1983 to Santarém, a city located at the meeting of the Amazon River and its tributary, the Tapajós, five hundred miles from Manaus.

Bea's mother again voiced her objection: "But your mother and daddy are now old. How can you leave us?"

Richard and Bea would be entering a phase of missionary service that would eventually involve the entire Walker family. It would touch the spiritual and physical lives of thousands of grateful residents along the Amazon and its tributaries. Surprisingly, however, it would arouse controversy and hostility from other missionaries residing in Belém, the urban giant five hundred miles away at the mouth of the Amazon, the Brazilian Baptist Home Mission Board, and from even the leadership of the Foreign Mission Board in Richmond, Virginia. But that subject is one for later discussion.

Chapter 12

This time the Walkers would be headed into a different situation. Santarém, their new location, was five hundred miles down river from Manaus, where they had served for ten years. No missionary had been serving in Santarém for seven years and the work was all but abandoned. For the first time, they would be without either of their sons, who remained in the States.

The Walkers felt honored that God would call them to this important position and soon learned to love the city and the people, who were very receptive to the Gospel.

The work in Santarém and the lower Amazon region was going well, but Bea's father back in the States became seriously ill. Her brother had died several years previously of cancer and she was the only living child. Her father's doctor called one night and said, "Bea, your parents need you. Your daddy is sick and your mother is so frail. You need to think about coming home." So the Walkers began to search for a time when they could return to the States.

Soon after their return to Brazil, they had become involved in a three-year cooperative plan with the Arkansas State Baptist Convention in which volunteer groups from Arkansas Baptist churches were organizing volunteer missionaries under the direction of Glendon Grober, a former cohort in Brazil, to go to the Lower Amazon River Valley. The program was known as the Amazon-Arkansas Partnership, or AMAR.

Carroll Caldwell, a former college classmate of Richard's and Director of Missions in southwest Arkansas, would take his initial trip with Richard from May 6 to 12, 1985. This trip would be an exploratory one and was a far cry from later ones in which groups would build churches, church educational additions, homes for national pastors; conduct Vacation Bible schools and revival services; and provide medical, dental, and optometry services.

In visits to Monte Alegre, Lake Paracarí, and Óbidos, Carroll was able to see needs that would help him to organize the Arkansas volunteers effectively. Richard preached at services or showed the two-hour "Jesus Film," provided by Parnell and Bonnie Swink of West Palm Beach, Florida. This couple had also given funds for a boat valuable for use by the Santarém churches in the river outreach ministry.

At Santa Rita, the group coordinated plans for the arrival of a volunteer group from Beech Street Baptist Church in Texarkana, Arkansas. At the Santa Rita church, people began to tell Richard and Carroll about how the people had been talking in tongues. Richard found only one or two who were radical in that they thought everyone should receive the gift of talking in tongues.

The church service here began at 8:00 P.M. and everything was proceeding well until one person began to lead in prayer. The orderliness ceased and everyone began to pray and praise at the same time.

Later, Richard was called upon to pray. Before he did, however, he explained, with as much love and care as he could, that if they were not going to hear what he said, there was no need for him to pray. There were "Amens" and everyone remained quiet while he prayed. He and Carroll later discussed with them the gifts of the Holy Spirit.

The missionaries went ashore early the next morning to talk with the leaders of the church about plans for the visit of the group from Texarkana. Then they were off on a two-hour trip to Jurutí where they found Senhor Birilo, moderator of the church. He called the workers together and they, too, made plans for a visit from the Texarkana group.

The mission trip of the seven-member group from May 22 to June 7, 1985, was something of a dress rehearsal for future missions with even wider scope. For Richard, many of the occurrences were similar to those he had encountered on other river trips, but for the seven volunteers, it was the experience of a lifetime. The pioneer team consisted of Dr. J. W. L. Adams, pastor; Randy Cofield, forest ranger; Dr. Karlton Kemp, physician; Ed May, realtor and investor; Tom Marshall, owner of a medical supply firm; Dr. John Thane, dentist; and Wayne Williams, college professor. Dr. Adams recorded the trip in his diary.

The team arrived in Santarém at 6:30 P.M. on May 22 and was greeted by Richard and Bea, who had prepared dinner in their missionary home. Crossing the street to the launch at 9:00 P.M., the team began their long journey upriver to the mission churches.

The group settled down for sleep about 11:00 P.M., with four in two double bunks and the remainder on top on inflated mattresses or swinging hammocks. It grew so intensely dark that the launch stopped near the riverbank at 3:30 A.M. and the group waited until daybreak. Most of the team slept fitfully through the night as the launch rolled from side to side.

They decided to have two cooked meals a day: breakfast and dinner. They would snack at lunch. Accordingly, duties were divided so that some would be cooks while the others would wash dishes and sweep floors.

They turned off the Amazon into a narrow channel that paralleled the main river. When they reached the end of the channel that afternoon, they saw a large island just across the Amazon from the outlet. This was Santa Rita, their destination.

The little church was filled as the evening service began under the glow of one electric light from a generator. Two thirds of the crowd were children or youth, who sat toward the front on eight-inch-wide pew slats.

The service was begun by words from the moderator, a layman who served as pastor. With young men on the front row accompanying on guitars, the members engaged in congregational and duet singing. The moderator then introduced Richard, who introduced the mission team. Randy Cofield and John Thane gave their testimonies, followed by a sermon by Dr. Adams. Richard translated their messages into Portuguese for the audience. One girl of about eleven years old came forward in response to the invitation. After this, two sisters, age four and seven, sang. The meeting closed with a prayer.

The team arose the next morning to find the launch listing to the side because of a leak, but the Brazilian boat boy repaired it.

When they arrived at the Santa Rita mission church the following day, they observed two women and one man scraping away something with hoes. They suddenly realized that they were cleaning away the wet cow manure so that the services could be held there that night. Fortunately, no unpleasant odor remained by the time of the services, which consisted of showing the complete film of the life of Christ.

The group went up to the church the next morning at 7:00 in order to be ready for Sunday School at 8:30, followed by morning worship services. Then the doctor and the dentist set up offices to treat patients, while the others handed out clothing. The children swamped those handing out clothes, then eventually the adults came up to receive clothes.

Another full day was spent at Santa Rita in treating medical and dental patients and in holding evening services. After treating three medical patients the next morning, the group headed upriver to Jurutí. Here they were given permission to plug in their extension cord so that they did not have to run their own generator from 5:00 P.M. to 11:00 P.M. They were surprised to find a number of different drugs in the local pharmacy. Six persons accepted Christ as Savior during the services.

Sudden downpours early the next two mornings drenched the group, which had already suffered from other rainstorms and from swarms of mosquitoes that had even gotten into the cabin. Since Dr. Thane was out of lidocaine and Dr. Kemp was weary, Richard suspended the clinics and the group inspected a city block that had been bought for the site of a church sanctuary.

A large group of church members gathered to say farewell as the group left Jurutí at 10:00 P.M. for a four-hour ride down river to Óbidos. Here they tarried only briefly before departing for Santarém. After having to pull into a cove in order to avoid a storm, the group arrived in Santarém at 3:00 P.M. on June 1.

Some elected to stay on the boat while others took hotel accommodations for two nights in Santarém. The group all attended 8:00 A.M. church services together at a church in Santarém on June 2, then went to evening services at the Aldeia (Village) Baptist Church where Richard was pastor and Bea was organist.

When the team reassembled at the airport early the next morning for departure, Dr. Thane, Ed, Tom, and Pastor Adams, who had stayed at the Hotel Tropical, were told that the launch had sunk during the night. Dr. Kemp, Wayne, and Randy, who had remained on board, had had to abandon ship when it was discovered sinking at 1:30 A.M. Nothing could be done to protect it as it sank to the bottom of the shallow water next to the pier. It was taken out of the water the next day, repaired, and was ready to go in time for the next trip.

Fifty-three professions of faith had been made during the trip in response to personal visitation and ten sermons preached. Many medical and dental problems had been treated. Richard and the Arkansas Baptist State Convention now knew that volunteer missionaries, even though they did not know the native language, could be of great benefit in not only ministering to physical needs, but in spreading the Gospel.

Chapter 13

Missionary Johnny Burnett came from Belém to assist in the organization of Igreja Batista de Porto Trombetes (Port Trumpets Baptist Church) from September 12 to 15, 1985. Also present were Richard Walker and Ronald Mathews, an independent Southern Baptist missionary from Óbidos. National pastors attending were Altair of Óbidos, Manoel Teixeira Jorge of Alenquer, Erivan of Orixíminá, and João Carlos of Santarém, a good representation of pastors in such a remote area. Richard preached to the thirty-six charter members of the new church on "Love and Prayer" from John 13:13–16.

Ten from the Central Baptist Church of Magnolia, Arkansas, arrived in Santarém on Monday, October 21. Six were to mix mud and mortar and lay blocks for much-needed additional educational space at the Aldeia Baptist Church that Richard pastored. The other four would convert a stall purchased in the new Mercadâo building into a Christian bookstore.

As Richard had already gathered much of the materials for construction, the crews soon got under way. Earl Pharr, a builder, was foreman of the group constructing the educational building. In addition to Earl, the group consisted of Ed Pharr, James Todd, Danny Bailey, veterinarian Don Impston, and Hal Harris.

Wayne Trull, an architect, was in charge of the bookstore team consisting of Art Duke, Wayne Griffith, and Miley Williams. Richard and Bea were kept busy running to and fro in order to furnish the two groups with materials and plenty of ice, tea, water, Cokes, and guaraná, a delicious Brazilian soft drink.

Joe Statton, minister of education for Central Baptist Church, arrived as the eleventh member of the team on Saturday, October 26. He had been doing a week-long clinic at the Belém seminary. He preached at the Aldeia church Sunday night, then led a clinic at the Aldeia church for the children's workers from the Santarém churches each day until Friday. The construction crews finished their tasks and all were ready for a day of relaxation, shopping, and packing on Friday.

Three men from Beech Street Baptist Church of Texarkana, participating in the AMAR project, came to Santarém from November 8 to 14 to help construct four rooms for additional church educational space at Jurutí. They did little construction but did enjoy visiting mission sites with Richard. Brazilian labor was hired to do the construction, and the building was dedicated on April 8, 1986.

A group mostly from the First Baptist Church of Jonesboro, Arkansas, stayed to work on building a parsonage at Monte Alegre down river from Santarém on January 8–21, 1986. Beth Ables, who recorded the trip, found it was to help her decide about whether she would go to a seminary and become a foreign missionary.

Primitive living conditions on the part of the Brazilians and the volunteer missionaries left a deep impression on Beth and her cohorts. Their wildest dreams came true when they boarded the two boats at Santarém that would take the group to Monte Alegre, a town of ten thousand inhabitants. Richard would take the mission boat that he had used years ago in the Amazonas field, *Eurico Nelson II*, and had rented another boat.

Beth soon learned to make up her hammock, but had difficulty getting into it. The kitchen was the size of a closet and the shower was the size of the kitchen. A square construction over the motor was used for a table. All of the women slept on the mission boat.

After arrival in Monte Alegre (Happy Mountain), the group was taken by the pastor, Artur Xabregas, up a steep hill to the building site. Concrete blocks had been stacked at the foot of the hill. The group of thirteen Arkansans, plus Missionary Richard and Pastor Xabregas, ate lunch on a long table placed on the outside of a church member's home. Beth could smell the outhouse as she dined.

The women pitched into the physical labor along with the men. A total of fifteen hundred concrete blocks were moved in one day. Although smaller than the North Americans, the natives were strong and could carry the blocks better than many of the American men.

Twice the group went into the jungle to cut poles for construction. The first time was rather scary for some of the women, who were oppressed by heat, humidity, and hordes of mosquitoes in the dense tropical jungle. Vines wrapped around the tree trunks made it hard to cut the poles. The second trip was different as the group rode into the jungle in a truck.

In addition to their construction work, they participated in worship services at Monte Alegre and at Aldeia Baptist Church in Santarém. Some gave testimonies and one preached, with Richard translating each. Beth marveled at the large number of people who could read the Bible in Portuguese without hesitation, and at the skill of an ten-year-old Brazilian girl who taught a Sunday School class.

Richard Walker designed and supervised the construction of this mission launch, the *Apostle*, in 1986. The boat was made possible by gifts from members of the First Baptist Church of West Palm Beach, Florida.

One couple took two crates, each weighing more than two hundred pounds, back with them to the States. Inside were two handcarved Brazilian model boats.

Four from the First Baptist Church of Benton, Arkansas, set out with Richard and Boyd on February 24 for a week-long maiden cruise in *The Apostle* to Porto Trombetas. Some preferred to call it "the shakedown cruise." The new boat, funded by members of the West Palm Beach, Florida, First Baptist Church, had been officially inspected and passed by the captain of the Port of Santarém. It was powered by a six-cylinder, 168-horsepower Mercedes diesel engine. It also had enough generators for navigation and inside lights, and to use for construction work along the Amazon. It contained a gas stove and refrigerator. The boat was deeply appreciated by the missionaries because the *Eurico Nelson II*, although it had served well for many years, was no longer safe to use.

This was the first trip in years in which Richard would have the able assistance of his son Boyd. The younger Walker had broken his arm and was not able to work at his regular job for several weeks, so his dad had encouraged him to help in the Amazon. Being the only missionaries on the field, Richard and Bea were feeling the need for reinforcements.

All went well during the first two hours on the maiden voyage until water was discovered in the hold of the boat. The bilge pump didn't work, so the four passengers went to work on the hand pump, while Richard managed to repair the bilge pump in forty-five minutes. Discounting the down time, they arrived in Óbidos in eight and a half hours as opposed to the ten hours it had taken in the *Eurico Nelson II*.

After less than an hour of sleep, Richard took the wheel at 11:30 P.M. to guide the launch through the Trombetas River, which had less trash than usual. Even though it hit two small logs during the night, the boat was undamaged. Having to steer the launch at night was like driving a car in a heavy rain. They docked at Oriximiná at 3:45 A.M.

The group had little time for sleep, however, as Pastor Eriván Miranda brought a dozen patients to Dr. Paul Hogue, physician, and Dr. Michael Bourns, dentist, at 7:00 A.M.

After treating the patients for two hours, the group took off for a little church on Carimú, a lake about two miles upriver. When they arrived at the church at 11:30 A.M., no one was waiting since the word had failed to get through that they were coming. They got into the jon boat and traveled from house to house, announcing over a loudspeaker that a doctor and dentist were available to treat patients.

They set up medical facilities in the unfinished temple and soon had a large crowd. Thinking that they had treated everyone, the physician and dentist were ready to load their equipment into the launch when two more canoes filled with patients arrived. The two doctors had to work until 8:00 P.M. before they were able to eat the delicious fried catfish, hush puppies, and French fries prepared by Austin Fikes, a retired executive from ALCOA.

Church services had to be held a little later that night than the planned 8:00 P.M. The Americans sang two songs, three from the group gave their testimonies, and Dr. Randel Everett, pastor of First Baptist Church of Benton, preached. Two said they were accepting Christ, but did not come forward.

As they moved from place to place, both the doctor and the dentist put in exhausting days as patients were lined up waiting as early as 6:30 A.M. In addition, the group held church services at 8:00 each night.

The alternator was acting up when the group prepared to depart for Santarém, but they decided to try to make it home. It seemed to have gone out completely when they were only two hours from home, but after some work and much prayer, it started again. They managed to limp into port at Santarém on March 2.

Once again, the trip had demonstrated the advantage of extending the healing hand as well as the hand of evangelism. The crowds had been drawn by the needs met by the physician and dentist, and Richard had seen the possibilities for an optometrist as through trial and error he fitted some eyeglasses on some patients. In addition to the many sick persons helped, the teeth extracted, or the eyeglasses fitted, fifteen souls had been added to the Kingdom and many had rededicated their lives. All had seen that someone really cared.

Five more volunteer groups would come during 1986, with the last one in August. The Walkers would return to the United States in August, also.

God was already preparing for future mission work through the coming of these groups during the AMAR Partnership. He drew Boyd into the circle because of a broken arm. Then He led Winston to work for the summer as he was out of school. The larger plan of

God for the Walker family's involvement in the Amazon Valley was unfolding.

Three men—a pastor, an insurance agent, and a retired forester—from Hope, Arkansas, arrived on March 18 to build a sanctuary for a church at Tapará, a mission of the Aldeia Baptist Church and across the river from Santarém. Diarrhea was the usual complaint among volunteers, but the exact opposite was true among two of the volunteers. Richard solved the problem with Tabasco sauce.

The group had almost finished laying the floor for the sanctuary before they had to prepare for their departure at 7:00 P.M. on March 24.

A group of four from Central Baptist Church of Magnolia, including a physician and a dentist, came as volunteers, staying from April 7 to 18. These traveled to Jurutí, Igarapé Açu, Santo Antonio in Lago Grande, Igarapé de Salé, and Carumú-Curí.

Leaving Santarém at 4:30 on the morning of April 8, the crew was navigating well until 5:15 A.M. In the short time that Boyd Walker was turning the wheel over to the boat boy, the ten-ton launch hit a sixty-foot log. Boyd was able to brace himself, but his hand was severely cut as it broke through and shattered the nearby glass. Dr. Tom Pullig wanted to stitch the cut, but Boyd decided to let him wrap the hand instead. Fortunately, the launch was not damaged even though the log was three feet in diameter and the launch speed was twelve miles per hour.

At Jurutí the group inspected the newly constructed Sunday School rooms and the *J. Adams* boat made possible by Pastor Adams and the Beech Street Baptist Church of Texarkana.

Three adolescents made professions of faith at the evening service. Then the congregation surprised Richard with a complete service for eight, a set of pottery made in Jurutí. He knew that Bea would be quite pleased. After dedication of the *J. Adams* missionary boat, the group returned to the new Sunday School rooms to cut a cake in celebration of the church's sixty-third anniversary. God had richly blessed this church with lay leadership, as they had never had a pastor during its long history.

Despite their tiring day, the group was up at 5:00 A.M. and soon headed toward Lago Grande and a place called Igarapé Açu. They went as far as they could in the launch, and then the rest of the way in the aluminum jon boat. The people waiting on the banks for them greeted them with Portuguese singing to the tune of "The Battle Hymn of the Republic."

The supplies were dumped into an ox cart for a hot thirty-minute haul. The doctor and dentist went right to work and by 1:30 P.M. the doctor had seen many patients and the dentist had extracted thirty teeth. Boyd did all of the translating for the doctor. The group then stopped to eat a tasty lunch of spaghetti prepared by the local women.

The next day a man came by with some tambaque, a delicious fish, and the missionaries purchased them for the women to cook for lunch. That gave the group enough energy to work until 5:00 P.M., then the doctor made two house calls, while the dentist labored on until 6:00 P.M. A total of fifty-seven patients were treated and one hundred teeth pulled.

A different perspective was provided on another mission, one lasting a month, from May 17 to June 16, provided by Camille Davis. This young unmarried woman reported on the activities of the group of students sponsored by the Arkansas Baptist Student Union.

Camille recorded all of the excitement of anticipating being used by the Lord in His service. Despite air sickness and customs difficulties when their translator left, she was still thrilled by the sight of children cutting bananas off the stalk, Brahma bulls pulling carts, and boats loaded with fish.

"This scenery we're passing is absolutely *beautiful*," Camille wrote after the group had begun its boat trip to Curumú-Vurí. "We just passed a huge farm which is owned by the man who got us our beef for the trip. The lake we have been travelling is Lago Grande. It's really big. We're traveling lakes and such so that we don't have to fight against the Amazon current."

Winston Walker, who had arrived with this group to spend the summer working with his parents, took Camille and Dianne fishing. Camille said she caught two piranhas, but admitted that they flopped off the hook. In addition, she became sea (or river) sick.

She reveals a bit of Richard Walker's caring, solicitous nature when she commented, "Richard, Boyd, and Winston are *invaluable*.

Richard's a sweet man! He's especially sweet to Dianne and me. He's never had a daughter, so he has a soft spot, I guess."

Camille expressed the feelings of visitors before her and the many who would follow when she wrote in her diary, "Thank You, Lord! I'm so glad You chose me!!"

Richard was sick with allergies, then influenza, during much of the first part of the trip. Boyd, too, was hit with influenza.

Camille joined the others in carrying and putting up wallboards, but her chief task was sweeping out the sawdust. Later on, she would assist in Bible school. Services were held nightly, with some of the services consisting of showing the life of Christ film in Portuguese.

The group left for Alenquer on June 6, with Boyd remaining in Santarém. On the way, they came to the meeting of the waters of the blue Tapajós and the sandy Amazon rivers at Santarém. They continued on the Amazon. Homesickness and the lack of privacy hit Camille hard while in Alenquer. She also felt frustrated because she could not communicate in Portuguese.

On June 11, the group moved on to Paracarí, where the other boat, the *Hilary*, was waiting with the wood for the church building. As the boat could not pull close enough to shore to unload, the wood was floated toward shore; then the natives scooped it up, put it on their heads, and carried it ashore. Meanwhile, the Arkansans were busy using machetes to clear the land for the building. A bunch of wasps forced one of the men, who was badly allergic to insect bites, to retire temporarily.

One of the native women took Camille and her friends to her house some fifteen minutes into the jungle. On the way she saw giant fanlike plants and a cactus some twenty feet tall. The woman gave them red peppers, tangerines, lemons, and a pineapple, all from out of her yard.

By June 15, Camille had learned to take a bath like a Brazilian. She donned her bathing suit, jumped into the lake from the top of the boat, swam around for a while, then soaped up again after getting back into the boat. She jumped into the lake again. She found the experience exhilarating.

Her summarizing comment after she flew home on June 16 was, "Man, I miss Brazil. I'm glad to be home, but when I think of those little children who would bring a canoe 45 minutes across the lake just for a balloon, or the ladies who would come all that way for a little plastic necklace, I get *sad* for them and wish I could go back and help them. I do miss the people there. It's kind of hard to normalize after that. I wish many times I was back there."

The next trip would prove crucial in the life work of the Walkers. Not only would it be their last mission trip that year before they returned to the States in August, but it would produce the seeds for the future Amazon Mission Organization.

Twenty-one members from the First and Second Baptist churches of Arkadelphia, Arkansas, made the trip to Paracarí from June 16 to 26 along with Richard, Winston, Boyd, three Brazilian women who served as cooks, and three Brazilian crewmen. Helen Thompson of the Second Baptist Church recorded the trip in her diary.

The group reached Paracarí after a three-hour ride on the rented boat, *Viageiro III,* down the Amazon from Santarém. Work began early on June 17.

> The lumber boat arrived this morning [Helen wrote]. Carts drawn by Brahma bulls were waiting to haul the lumber to the work site where much of the original construction was begun last week by two carpenters from Richard's church in Santarém. This includes floor joists and some side wall framing.
>
> Men, women, and children are gathered by the boat, or walk from the little village, anxiously awaiting to watch or to assist in unloading the lumber. The people are excited as much as we are who came here to help do this job. The carts are pulled about half a mile to the construction site.

The medical and dental teams set up their clinics in the school building. The two nurses, Jim and Maggie Payne, along with Boyd, saw twenty-five patients, and gave out medication for parasites, pain, and skin and female problems. They treated such problems as prostatitis, high blood pressure, and breast lumps.

Meanwhile, Dr. Jim Hankins and assistant Kristi Hagan extracted a number of teeth, while the Vacation Bible School volunteers worked with an enthusiastic group of fifty-five youngsters.

Helen described a Brazilian home she visited that afternoon:

"... a home that was immaculate with a dirt floor, very primitive kitchen (though with plenty of utensils), one bedroom with two hammocks for the children, and bed built in one corner. A family of five share this bedroom.

In the living room, there were two small benches, a shelf with a suitcase on it, a sewing machine somewhat like we see in the U.S. (used also as a table and with a treadle), a table with a small black and white TV which is covered to keep dust off it.

They seem to be very happy with their lifestyle. The lady of this house is also the seamstress of the village.

After work, all of the group walked up and down the sandy trails to make sure everyone knew that services would be held at 7:30 that night. Despite only two showers, all twenty-four managed to get their baths before service, which consisted of a sermon by Bill Dixon and testimonies, with congregational singing and special music. Alberto Gomez, a Brazilian student from Ouachita Baptist University in Arkadelphia, did the translating for the sermon and testimonies.

After services, the visiting group gathered in the boat for devotional time, led the first night by Jim and Maggie Payne. Then down went the air mattresses, up went the hammocks, and others went to bunks. They went to sleep to a lake breeze that would chill them all before morning.

The work progressed on schedule, despite the fact that nearly all of the group suffered at least some mild form of illness during the trip. The group swam blithely in the lake until they were told the natives did not swim there for fear of the man-eating piranhas!

The final night of their stay arrived on June 25. Helen wrote:

Tonight's service was a real highlight of our trip. The building was beautiful with flowers on a tablecloth-draped table. People poured in; 264, not counting lap babies, were counted. The sanctuary, windows, and porches were full of people, with many more standing in the yard.

Much singing, message by Bill Dixon, installation of the evangelist for this mission church, special music, presentation of Bibles to the church and to the village leaders, presentation of American and Christian flags, all made up a two-hour meeting.

Six ladies marched up with six bouquets of flowers for the

American ladies. . . . After the service, at least 150 people—men, women, and children—came by to hug and kiss us (some crying). This is a sad day for us, but a glorious one for the Lord.

During the eleven days, a total of eight sermons had been preached, with 12 public decisions, 428 patients seen by the medical team, 486 teeth extracted by the dentists, and more than 100 children attending Vacation Bible School. The supply of eyeglasses was exhausted before the end of the third day.

In addition, the group, including the Brazilian cooks and crewmen, were treated twice to banana pudding prepared by Helen Thompson. But most importantly, members of the Arkadelphia group got off the plane in Arkansas talking about the next trip they would take to Brazil.

The last group of three from First Baptist Church of Arkadelphia came within days of the previous team that labored in Paracarí. Dr. Raymond Coppenger and wife, Agnes, and Dr. Carl Goodson arrived to teach in the Laymen's Institute held at the Aldeia Baptist Church in Santarém. The two men were retired professors of Ouachita Baptist University, and Agnes was retired head of the Alumni Association there. The three held daily classes for many lay persons, both men and women, who did not tire of learning during the two-week session.

Even with the volunteer groups arriving on the field each month, Bea's principal responsibility was with the Aldeia Baptist Church that Richard pastored in Santarém. She was organist and there was an active choir with weekly choir rehearsals. She was also leader of an enthusiastic Young Women's Auxiliary and was involved in Woman's Missionary Union activities.

Chapter 14

The Walkers had only four months accrued on a furlough when they returned to Arkansas because of the failing health of Bea's dad and the strain on her mother. When that time was up, however, nothing was any better regarding the health of Mr. Rodgers, and her mother still needed them desperately.

They felt that they could not return to Brazil at this time, but AMAR projects had already been scheduled for the Amazon through the Arkansas Baptist State Convention. Since these would have to be cancelled unless they could accompany the groups, the Walkers were put on loan to the Arkansas State Convention by the Foreign Mission Board in Richmond.

Bea's father died in March 1987, but the Walkers realized that the real problem was with Mrs. Rodgers, who was unable to cope in her frail condition. They continued to work with AMAR in accompanying the volunteer groups while residing in Arkansas.

After nearly five months away from Brazil, Richard finally returned to the Lower Amazon Basin February 4, 1987, to visit the churches in Santarém and other churches and missions to which he had ministered during his river trips. By doing so, he was better able to coordinate the work to be done by future volunteer groups from Arkansas.

Returning to his missionary home in Santarém, he found the house, boat, and car in excellent condition. João Carlos was the only Baptist minister left in Santarém, a city of 125,000 with five Baptist churches and seven strong missions. Naturally, he was overworked.

Since he was the only Baptist pastor in Santarém, Pastor João Carlos dreamed of starting a Bible Institute for young people and older adults to prepare for the leadership jobs in the churches. He wished to build it on the new Baptist camp property, which the University Baptist Church of Fayetteville, Arkansas, had given to Richard for that purpose.

João hoped the students would raise fish and rabbits, along with other things, to support themselves. The students would vacate the property for a month at the end of each three months. During the time that they were gone home, the property could be used for retreats or for other purposes.
    Richard renewed old friendships and made plans for the future as he briefly visited each place. One Brazilian family reminded him of his own large number of brothers and sisters. When he asked a man how many children he had, he replied that he had twelve, but could come up with only eleven names. He finally realized which one was missing.
    Richard made it to Belém on time on February 18, but he was unable to get on the VARIG flight to the United States. He stayed with the Orman Gwynns for several days and then flew on to Manaus, the site of his first Brazilian pastorate. After many delays, he flew to Miami on March 1 and was met at the airport by Bea.
    Many things about this trip puzzled and even frustrated Richard. The long delay in getting a flight to the States bothered him, but it gave him time for much prayer, meditation, and study.

    This trip was followed by a medical team trip from April 23 to May 27 to Arapiúns and Monte Sião. The team members consisted of Dr. Hank Jordan, physician, and Dr. Lester Barrett, dentist, both from Jonesboro, Arkansas; Dr. Larry Brandenberg, dentist, and his wife, Libby, dental assistant, from Rising Sun, Maryland; Judy Alkema R.N. and Mary Ann Holbrook R.N. from Greenville, South Carolina; and Dr. and Mrs. Raymond Coppenger of Arkadelphia, Arkansas. Bea Walker stayed in Santarém to take care of the visas before flying back to the States.
    The group sailed from Santarém at midnight but traveled only an hour up the Tapajós River before docking. Immediately, a heavy rainstorm hit. Leaving their haven at 5:30 A.M., they spent three and a half hours crossing the river. They had elected not to cross the wide and dangerous river at night.
    Entering the mouth of the Arapiúns River, they traveled another five hours to Monte Sião (Mount Zion) and arrived around noon on Sunday, April 26. The people had expected the group on the previous Friday, but gave them a warm welcome. The medical team went right

to work, seeing people before church that evening. With excellent response to the preaching of Dr. Coppenger, and with the medical and dental teams tending to the usual large number of patients, the trip was marked up as a highly successful one.

The Arkansas-Amazon cooperation (AMAR) was scheduled to terminate at the end of 1987. A group from the First and Second Baptist churches of Arkadelphia had another AMAR trip scheduled in June and July, but a number of them did not want the volunteer missionary work in Brazil to end. A group headed by Sherwin and Wanda Williams and Bill and Snookie Dixon approached Boyd Walker with the idea of heading up an organization that would continue the volunteer missionary work in Brazil. They offered to pay him a salary.

Boyd got his chance to find out what it would be like to run such an organization when he took over for Richard in making all of the preparations for the AMAR trip by the Arkadelphia group. Richard and Bea had thought that Boyd would operate such an organization while living in the United States and taking care of his grandmother. They would continue their missionary service, living in Santarém, thereby enabling those groups that desired to continue their partnership program.

One can imagine his surprise when, visiting Col. John Brink and his wife, Virginia, in Salem, Arkansas, Richard received a call from an irate Foreign Mission Board staff member who demanded that he kill the burgeoning organization that Boyd was forming. Otherwise he and Bea could not return to Brazil as Southern Baptist missionaries.

Richard thought the call was ridiculous since he had taken no part in the organization of the Amazon Mission Organization (AMOR), formed in August 1987, other than to advise his son how not to come into conflict with what was being done by Southern Baptists.

The Walkers thought that Boyd was undertaking a noble task. When the Foreign Mission Board refused to have anything to do with AMOR, Richard and Bea had no alternative but to resign from the Board and take care of her mother. Their original plan had been dissolved by others.

After a letter or two was exchanged between Richard and Area Director Dr. Bill Richardson, the Walkers resigned in April 1988. With the official "letter of regret," they received their fifteen-year service pins from the Board. Because of the need of attention by Bea's mother, many thought that her frailty was the only reason for their withdrawal from the foreign mission field when in reality they felt they had been given no other choice.

Boyd found the task of preparing for a volunteer mission trip was a tremendous one. After arriving in Santarém on May 24, along with his brother Winston, he wrote of their first day: "It's been a challenging day—much flying, much waiting, very taxing. The 'old emotions' are active as well. Regardless of how much we plan and prepare for these trips, the reality of it all is sobering. So, after praying for strength, patience, and perseverance, we're on our way."

After sleeping all the next day, Boyd was rejuvenated and enjoyed the sounds and smells of the Latin city. He also renewed acquaintances with former friends. He soon ran into difficulty as he found out that "instant" transfer of money in Brazil meant waiting forty-eight hours. Each day he would shop at ten different stores in order to get the best prices. He also bargained with some merchants in order to pay at that day's price for something to be delivered next week, knowing that it would be 30 percent higher then.

In addition to renting a boat or boats for the Arkadelphia group, he had to be sure that they were well stocked with food and supplies. He also had to purchase the lumber for the building at Alenquer.

Boyd found it hard to switch from U.S. to Brazilian methodology, but he began to practice praying in Portuguese. It renewed him spiritually to attend Aldeia Baptist Church in Santarém again even though it was now pastorless. Talking by telephone with his dad in the States helped give him encouragement and guidance.

Winston, too, was an important partner with Boyd. After twenty-five days of preparation, they were looking forward eagerly to the arrival of the Arkadelphia group. They got the boats docked in front of the missionary house on Thursday morning, May 28, and loaded supplies from 9:30 A.M. until 6:30 P.M. The Arkadelphia group, including Richard, arrived at 7:20 P.M. Richard would remain somewhat in the background while Boyd ran the operation, but Boyd knew that he could count on his father for timely advice. The group boarded the three boats—the *Apóstolo, Hilary,* and *Cisne*—for Paracarí at 11:30 P.M.

They arrived in Baheiras at 11 the next morning and were met by a waiting crowd, including a man named Amedio, the patriarch of the community. The medical groups set up in the dance hall and were soon treating patients, pulling teeth, and examining eyes. In three hours they had given fifty "physicals," pulled twenty-seven teeth, and made fifty eye examinations.

When the group was ready to anchor offshore that night, it discovered that the *Apóstolo* was stuck in the mud on the riverbank. In the process of freeing the boat, the crew ripped a piece of caulking out of the hull and the *Apóstolo* began to leak profusely. Paulo, the boat boy, was not happy about having to go into the water at night to repair the leak, but no sooner had he stopped the leak then the generator burned out. An exasperated Boyd, however, did get his dinner and got to bed by 9:00 P.M.

The medical teams worked through the noon hour, barely taking time to grab a bite to eat, since they needed to be in Alenquer before night. Here they would have a reunion with the main group from Arkadelphia. Boyd wrote, "I had the strangest feeling . . . seeing all of these friends together in Alenquer, of all places!"

The next day the group headed back into the interior toward the Paracarí area. After they had settled down for showers, dinner, and devotional, the group had what Boyd called "a great discussion about the continuation of this type of medical ministry even in the absence of a partnership such as AMAR. I look forward to more discussion about same . . . "

The days were long and arduous as the medical teams usually began their work at 8:00 A.M. and worked until late afternoon. Sometimes there were home visits. The nurse anesthetist, Clyde Temple, had to open up an infected leg of a little boy who had broken his leg some four months earlier and had received no medical attention. Boyd thought that the lad would either lose his leg or his life within a short time.

The Americans took up an collection to send him to Santarém for surgery and were to take him the following day. The boy's father became suspicious that they were going to take the child away from him, so the family left in the darkness that night for their home. Clyde Tempel also removed a fatty tumor from a woman's head.

Even Sunday did not keep the medical teams from carrying out their tasks. On Sunday, June 28, those in the *Apóstolo* had to go to Jarací to check on some patients. Charlie Hartsfield, one of the dentists, wanted to do surgery on a small girl, but needed Clyde to anesthetize her. She had become hysterical the day before.

When they arrived, however, they found that she had ridden two hours back home on horseback and would be back at 5:00 P.M. Clyde sedated her with Valium and Ventanyl, then Charlie pulled the teeth that had abscessed, with the abscess draining through the jaw and out underneath it.

Finally, on Wednesday, July 1, the Arkadelphia trip was completed and Boyd was able to pay off outstanding debts in Santarém. He had purchased what he thought was "gold" jewelry for the group, but found out that it was only gold-plated. He took it back and got a refund.

With the Arkadelphians and their dad gone, Boyd and Winston remained in Santarém for ten more days. Concerning the past forty days, Boyd wrote on July 2:

> 6 A.M. I am sitting here on the porch of the mission house watching the riverfront slowly come alive. I've had a little time these past few days to reflect on what all has transpired over these 40 days spent in the Santarém area. I really thank the Lord for giving me this unique opportunity. He has shown me a great deal about myself.
>
> I feel more comfortable with some areas of my life, and less with other areas. I don't believe I could come down here and sell the Baptist religion, or any other denomination, for that matter. I want to preach and teach Christ. THAT'S ALL! The Medical/Dental ministry seems to have really captured my heart. I wait anxiously for the Lord to open my eyes to His leadership in my life!

Boyd was glad to get a call from his dad that night, even though it awoke him from sleep. He found Richard supportive of his idea of buying the *Hilary* if it were available at the right price. Boyd thought he could buy and refurbish it for $35,000. When the price on the *Hilary* was listed at $50,000 and other boats were jacked up, however, Boyd decided it would be better to rent boats for the present time.

Meanwhile, Richard had become pastor of a small church in Lantana, Florida, and he and Bea were able to move back into their former home in West Palm Beach. Her mother left her Benton, Arkansas, home and moved with them to sunny Florida.

Although they would not become involved full time until May 17, 1988, Richard would go on all five AMOR trips of 1988 and would offer needed counsel to his sons.

The ten days Boyd and Winston spent at Santarém after the Arkadelphia group had left were busy ones. Boyd spent much time reflecting about what he should do in the future. He wrote: "The Lord is really dealing with me about my involvement here on the Amazon. But I feel very distant from Him. This MUST become my priority—to cut out more of the world and give Him total control. To be honest, I don't want the responsibility over my own life . . . "

They helped Paulo, the boat boy, and his family move out of the missionary house in preparation for the arrival of the new missionary family, the Bobby Leonards. Even though it had never been their home, it made him sad to see others taking over the house, car, and boat that his dad and mom had once used.

Even though the Leonards offered to let Boyd and Winston use the house until their furniture arrived, the two brothers were glad to stay in the Tropical Hotel to escape those who had begged money from them. When the Leonard furniture did arrive, eighty percent of it was damaged.

Boyd tried to explain to Bobby that his volunteer medical/dental ministry would not conflict with the work of Southern Baptists. He felt frustrated that Bobby did not comprehend how a medical/dental ministry would open doors for evangelism. He was also surprised that the "new wave" of missionaries were those serving for four-year terms instead of the former career missionary. He wondered whether many of them were more interested in building up their résumés rather than missionary careers.

On Day 47 of his stay in Brazil, Boyd wrote:

> I'm just going to have to get serious with the Lord about my vocation. I truly believe that He has been, and still is, preparing me for some sort of "permanence." I enjoy setting up for and taking these groups up and down the river—that part I like.

Over the past couple of weeks I've been trying to "play missionary." IT HASN'T WORKED! It's an entirely different ball game. I don't believe I like it. Scrounging around, trying to get things arranged for a "group" from the States is FAR different from trying to get a "good deal" for the church. I've fallen on my face a couple of times trying to do that.... When I talk to Dad, maybe he will give me some pointers dealing with this . . . "

On his final day in Santarém Boyd drew this conclusion: "These past few days were to be the reassuring boost that would lead me to KNOW that the mission field is where I need to be. Well, it doesn't seem to have worked! I WANT to be down here—but NOT in the missionary capacity! The way it stands right now, if the Lord wants me here, it will be as a hard-working layman. I don't see anything wrong with that, but it's not entirely what I had in mind at the onset."

So, by the time the Walker brothers boarded the plane at Manaus for Miami on July 12, Boyd had pretty well set his career course on volunteer missions as a layman.

Earlier on the final AMAR mission trip to the Lower Amazon region had come in August 1987. Richard had received a telephone call one morning informing him that a group of six men from north central Arkansas was scheduled to go to Brazil, but no one was available to take them. Richard said that he and Bea would gladly go.

They met their group for the first time at the Little Rock airport. The group consisted of Jess Taylor, director of missions for the Rocky Bayou Baptist Association, and five from Immanuel Southern Baptist Church of Salem: Mark Weaver, pastor; John Brink, retired Army colonel; Dr. Alan Winberry, dentist; and Gary Barker and Russell Perkins, both respiratory therapists.

They were divided into two groups in their evangelistic outreach in Itaituba on the Tapajós River. Richard was translator for one group, while Bea translated for the other group. Out of this experience, Dr. Winberry and Col. Brink were to become members of the Board of Directors of the Amazon Mission Organization, which would be organized just a month later.

Meanwhile, the AMAR Partnership Missions would be climaxed with a city-wide crusade in Manaus from October 22 to

November 1. A total of 190 Americans from 58 churches, along with 31 Manaus churches, were to be involved. One of the many American pastors was Richard Walker, who was one of seven translators.

Much advance preparation went into the crusade and 200,000 New Testaments in Portuguese were distributed. The soccer stadium was rented for three nights, with Nilson Finini, Brazil's "Billy Graham," preaching. Crowds during the respective three nights were approximately 16,000, 30,000, and 40,000.

Conversions could not all be counselled because of the scarcity of counselors. At least 4,000 made decisions for Christ, with some of these being the very wealthy citizens of Manaus. It is believed that during the entire campaign, including immediately before and after the Crusade, 9,555 persons made commitments to Christ.

The groundwork for the astounding crusade results, however, had been laid in the Lower Amazon region by the 19 different groups sent during the past two years of AMAR. Not only had these groups tended to the spiritual needs of the Amazon people, with more than 1,000 decisions for Christ resulting, but they had ministered to very real physical needs.

The dentists had extracted more than 3,300 teeth and were able to fill a few teeth with a small portable dental unit donated by Dr. Larry Brandenburg of Rising Sun, Maryland. Eye specialists had fitted at least 1,500 glasses, while the doctors' roles included anything from doing general health checkups to minor surgery. Most of these people in remote areas had received no previous medical, dental, or optometry service. Many had never heard the Gospel preached, at least in an evangelical manner.

Also important to the Partnership missions program were the construction teams that built eighteen structures, including churches, parsonages, and educational buildings.

Included as well were house-to-house visitations and preaching to small and large groups. Bible schools, Bible studies, and nutrition classes were offered. Through interpreters, leaders taught songs, told stories, and played games. Also, hundreds of Portuguese New Testaments were distributed.

The official AMAR project, however, ended with the Manaus Crusade, and the Arkansas Baptist State Convention would concentrate its efforts abroad in Guatemala for three years beginning with

1990. The vast Amazon Basin would be left with a few missionaries serving key cities such as Belém, Santarém, and Manaus, but the remote areas of the Amazon and its tributaries would be left untouched by the Foreign Mission Board.

Boyd Walker and his backers from the Arkadelphia First and Second Baptist churches, however, were determined to carry on the work that had yielded so many results in the past two years. He would soon be joined by the entire Walker family, and the Amazon Mission Organization (AMOR) would become a full-time family undertaking. Boyd, however, would carry the load as AMOR president for 1988 and would be ably assisted by Winston, who now lived in Santarém.

Chapter 15

With its city-wide crusade in Manaus in November 1987, the Southern Baptist Foreign Mission Board in Richmond had stirred the hearts of many pastors and laymen in the United States with zeal for volunteer missions. A total of 58 churches and 190 American volunteers were involved in the crusade. Unfortunately, leaders of the board, apparently fearing that "para church" groups would develop to take money away from the Cooperative Program, moved quickly to extinguish those fires.

Some opposition had been shown by some leaders of the board toward the Arkansas-Amazon Partnership Missions. Its opposition to AMOR and other volunteer groups was much more virulent.

The board wrote to twenty-five volunteer groups in May 1988 and invited them to meet with the board in February 1989. Meanwhile, AMOR faced hostility from the board, the Brazilian Baptist Home Mission Board, and missionaries in the Amazon Basin.

Despite the opposition from Richmond and from missionaries in Brazil, Boyd and Winston were able to organize and carry out four trips to the Lower Amazon region during 1988. A total of 103 volunteers began two new works, constructed three temples and one parsonage, while physicians saw 1,147 patients, dentists extracted 1,470 teeth, and eye specialists fitted 500 glasses. Most important, an average of 152 attended Vacation Bible School, 169 made professions of faith, and 12 were baptized.

Twenty-seven volunteers from the First Baptist Church of Murray, Kentucky, were the first to go, from July 3 to 13. Led by Dan Shipley, they erected a church building and started a new work in Barreiras on the Tapajós River, with 36 decisions and 13 baptisms. The medical team treated 397 and the dental team extracted 320 teeth.

Following soon after, a group of 32 volunteers from the First Baptist Church of Russellville, Arkansas, went to Soure on Marajo Island at the mouth of the Amazon River from July 17 to 27. Dr.

Stephen Davis, pastor, not only led this group but would lead other trips and would serve on the AMOR Board. This team had 68 decisions, extracted 850 teeth, saw 350 medical patients, fitted 500 eyeglasses, held Vacation Bible School, and distributed 1,500 Portuguese New Testaments.

Boyd Walker led 14 volunteers from Beech Street Baptist Church of Texarkana, Arkansas, and other area churches to Jurutí on the Amazon River from July 31 to August 10. They built a parsonage and ministered in the areas of medical, dental, Vacation Bible School, and evangelism. No statistics were kept.

Dr. Joe McKinney, pastor of Gracemont Baptist Church of Tulsa, Oklahoma, led 30 volunteers from his church on a trip to Itaituba on the Tapajós River from August 28 to Sept. 7. Here in the community of Transporto, this last group for 1988 began a new work, had 65 decisions, 17 baptisms, extracted 300 teeth, treated 400 medical patients, had 200 average attendance in Daily Vacation Bible School, and erected a church building.

Two of the churches, First Baptist of Russellville and Gracemont of Tulsa, would send volunteers on repeat missions in 1989.

Members of the AMOR Board saw the need of Richard and Bea's long experience in the Lower Amazon region in order to carry out the missions, despite the strong opposition that had already caused many other volunteer groups to abandon their efforts. The senior Walkers resigned from the First Baptist Church at Lantana, Florida, in time to join the first AMOR trip of 1989 by the First Southern Baptist Church of Del City, Oklahoma, to Aveiro on the Tapajós River from May 14 to 24.

The AMOR Board named Richard president and Boyd vice president for the organization. Sherwin Williams, owner of a computer consulting firm in Arkadelphia, Arkansas, served as chairman of the Board, while Bill Dixon, dean of students at Ouachita Baptist University, was secretary-treasurer for 1989.

Five from AMOR attended the February 1989 meeting in Richmond, Virginia, to which they had been invited by the Foreign Mission Board. Sixteen other volunteer organizations of the twenty-five invited also attended and participated. AMOR members attending included Dr. Alan Winberry, Salem, Arkansas; Robbie Rudolph

The Walkers as they were at the beginning of AMOR (from left to right): Richard and Bea, Winston and Odemeia, and Boyd and Cida. Seven years later, by the end of 1994, the number of Walkers had increased to ten.

and Dan Shipley, Murray, Kentucky; and Boyd Walker and Bill Dixon of Arkadelphia, Arkansas.

The extended meeting allowed for visiting with Dr. Thurmon Bryant, associate vice-president for Volunteer Management; Ron N. Boswell, director of Volunteers in Missions Department; and Dr. John Cheyne, director of Human Needs Department. In each case, the purpose of AMOR was explained. Although each of these worked within the broad guidelines of the Foreign Mission Board, each was attentive and appreciative of the efforts of AMOR.

In the broader meeting, however, Dr. Keith Parks, Board President, reminded the participants that the policies of the Foreign Mission Board are established by the Southern Baptist Convention. Among those most pertinent, he said, is "the prohibition against directly raising funds through local churches or being connected to fund-raising activities in churches."

Parks continued by saying that "independent organizations, while led by Southern Baptists, are accountable to constituencies in local churches and not to the convention as a whole." Foreign Mission Board staff members asked the independent organizations to involve all who ultimately would be affected as they planned their overseas projects.

For the projects planned for 1989, AMOR had already sought levels of input from Pastor Eluardo, João Carlos, the Pará Baptist Convention in Brazil, the Brazil Home Mission Board, Bobby Leonard who was the Southern Baptist missionary in Santarém, and the Foreign Mission Board of the Southern Baptist Convention.

As a final note on the Richmond meeting, AMOR was instructed to list all of the needs as expressed through the chain of command above, to send these to the missionary in Santarém, and to ask for a project number. AMOR was told to proceed if paperwork delayed the issuance of such a number. AMOR agreed to do so and to send a report to the Foreign Mission Board on each of the trips made in 1989.

Richard preached a moving final message to the First Baptist of Lantana on Sunday, May 14; then Chuck Sumerlin took Bea and him to board the Varig airplane at Miami. Also aboard was a group from First Baptist Church of Del City, Oklahoma. It consisted of 26, with an optometrist, two dentists, two physicians, two registered nurses, a licensed practical nurse, ten evangelism/Vacation Bible School workers, and seven construction workers.

The group arrived in Belém at 12:30 A.M. with 42 pieces of luggage with proper consulate-approved documents to bring in medical and dental supplies, plus 750 pairs of used eyeglasses. The customs official, however, balked, so Richard cried, begged, argued, and showed about every conceivable emotion. The official was angry, but he relented and passed all the luggage without opening it! The volunteers sang the "Doxology" and "Amazing Grace" on the sidewalk just outside the customs office.

After an exhausting night, the group left Belém at 6:30 A.M. for the hour flight to Santarém. Here the Walkers got their first glimpse of their first grandchild, little Richard Edward Walker II, son of Winston and Odemeia. Since Winston's family and Boyd accompanied them, they did not leave Santarém for Aveiro until 1:00 P.M. for a ten-hour boat ride on the Tapajós River.

Bea helped set up the clinic and served as a nurse alongside two physicians, another nurse, and two translators. The licensed practical nurse worked as pharmacist. They would see 53 patients the first day, while the dentists extracted 62 teeth from the 24 persons they saw, the optometrist fitted 120 persons with glasses, and teachers instructed 150 persons in Daily Vacation Bible School. Richard preached at the night service in the partially completed building.

The work continued unabated throughout the week, with everyone up by daybreak and breakfast at 6:30 A.M. The medical team made house calls at 7:00 A.M., but Thursday morning started off at 4:30 A.M. when a pregnant woman being kept at the clinic went into labor. She delivered a boy at 5:30 and named him Timothy Albert after the first names of the two physicians. By Friday, the hectic pace was beginning to take its toll. Bea wrote:

> The Clinic becomes more of an impossibility every day! Sick, sick people. Today, we had a 15-year-old girl who came in with extremely high fever. The doctors think it might be meningitis, but have decided it's probably malaria. No way for lab tests here, so they have to treat by the old "gut feeling." A 17-month-old baby was brought in with renal failure. May lose him.
>
> Another baby arrived with pneumonia—his little brother died yesterday with exactly the same symptoms. We treated him Monday.

These three patients are in our "Infirmary" and on I.V. fluids. We saw a two-year-old with cerebral palsy, a case of mumps, and a case of whooping cough.

Only one physician was at the clinic since the other was away at a gynecological clinic. The eye clinic was closed early because the optometrist became ill. A dentist was exhausted, so Boyd helped pull teeth. Daily Vacation Bible School workers were swamped with 450 children.

The physicians were up most of Friday night treating the sick. A person came to the boat at midnight seeking help for a woman who had suffered a heart attack. Bea and the other registered nurse did intensive care unit duty from 7:30 A.M. until 1:30 P.M.

The young parents of the seventeen-month-old boy who was being treated for pneumonia decided to take their son home "to die in peace" since they could not afford the blood transfusions needed at the hospital in Santarém. The volunteer medical team sadly agreed that this would be best. The other two infirmary patients were well enough to be sent home.

The medical team continued its work through Saturday and was touched when sick people told them that they would keep their numbers in line until the team returned next year if the doctors could not see them on this trip. This alone was enough motivation for the team to continue its work on Sunday afternoon after a baptismal service Sunday morning.

The Walkers' grandson, little Ricardo, was dedicated at the night service. The mayor spoke and Richard preached. The Brazilians liked the fact that the Walkers' daughter-in-law and grandson were Brazilians.

The group had barely settled in on the boat after the Sunday night service when a young couple brought a three-year-old girl to the boat. The girl was very distended and quite ill. Melinda, a translator, started to carry the baby to the clinic, but the child died in her arms. Richard was up past midnight, helping to make arrangements for burial.

The medical team was again awakened early Monday morning to deliver a full-term, two-and-a-half-pound girl. Nurse Tammy Flowers delivered her and the parents named the baby Tammy Rhonda (Traue) after the two nurses. The volunteers sailed from

Aveiro at noon Monday. One of the women became deathly seasick on the trip back to Santarém, but fortunately none of the boats had mechanical problems. When the group got to Santarém, it learned that the seventeen-month-old boy had died only a few hours after his parents got him home on Saturday.

Tuesday was a shopping day for the group, then all were up at 4:30 A.M. and were at the airport at 6:30 A.M., but the plane did not leave until 9:30. It had been difficult for the Walkers to say "goodbye" to their new grandson, but the parting was eased by the fact that they would be returning within a month. The Varig plane in Belém was loaded and waiting, so the volunteers got on board and were in Miami in six hours.

Statistics were not the consuming interest, but they did tell a part of the story. These included 438 average attendance in Daily Vacation Bible School, 420 patients seen by the physicians, 584 teeth extracted, 459 glasses fitted, 62 decisions in church services and 65 during home visits, 3 baptisms with others waiting, and a completed and dedicated new temple of worship. The work was left in the hands of two new converts and the occasional visits of the nearest Brazilian pastor and a lay evangelist.

The work in Aveiro was the first ever Baptist witness there even though the town was a county seat. The Walkers hoped that the many Brazilians who had come from up and down the Tapajós River and from settlements in the interior would share the Gospel with their neighbors.

For many Arkadelphians from the First and Second Baptist churches, the trip to Brasilia Legal on the Tapajós River from June 25 to July 5 would be their third or fourth trip to Brazil. It would have special significance to such first-timers as your author, however, since it would be his first and only AMOR trip.

Probably the most surprising element was the amount of advance preparation that was necessary long before the actual trip. Volunteers from both churches began meeting each Sunday afternoon starting early in 1989 under the experienced leadership of Bill Dixon. Each of the volunteers was asked to prepare a one-page testimony, which would be translated by Brazilians or children of missionaries to Brazil.

Other volunteers took on committee responsibilities such as publicity, soliciting prayer partners, and obtaining visas. In addition to choosing a time to give their testimonies, the volunteers picked a night to give a bedtime devotional to the group while in Brasilia Legal.

Given the option, the group chose to fly to Rio de Janeiro for two days after completing the work in Brasilia Legal. Most of the group members carried their luggage down to the First Baptist Church on Saturday night so that it could be weighed, tagged, and loaded onto the church bus, which would carry the Arkadelphians to the airport in Little Rock early Sunday morning. Eighteen volunteers met the Walkers in Miami for the flight to Belém, while Sherwin and Wanda Williams took an earlier flight to Rio to meet Boyd's wife, Cida, and to assist the Brazilian Home Mission Board in setting up a computer system.

Many of the group would find that the most difficult part of the mission was enduring the long trip to Brasilia Legal. After arrival in Belém around midnight, the group wandered around the airport all night or worked with Helen Thompson in filling balloons with Scripture verses.

The excited volunteers boarded the plane for Santarém on time at 6:30 A.M., but after sitting on board a hot plane for forty-five minutes, they deplaned when the crew could not make the air conditioning work. After two more hours in the airport, they boarded a plane for a 65-minute ride to Santarém.

Boyd met the group at Santarém and Winston came later. Odemeia and little Ricardo were already on the boat. Finally, the exhausted group of eighteen, plus seven members of the Walker family, left Santarém at 1:00 P.M. for the twelve-hour boat ride up the Tapajós River to Brasilia Legal. In addition to ten crew members, a woman to do the laundry, and kitchen help, a young man named Daniel came from the Brazilian Home Mission Board to observe the work and to make a video tape.

Even the hammock felt comfortable to your author as it was the first time after many exhausting hours that he and most of the group could stretch out almost horizontally. He had lain down briefly on a bench at the Belém airport, but had lost his place when he arose to telephone his missionary niece in Bela Horizonte.

If the newcomers had expected a small river because the Tapajós was a tributary, they were surprised to learn that it was much wider than the mighty Mississippi River, was more than 1,000 miles long, and carried 80,000-ton ships compared to the 10,000-ton limit on the Mississippi. The beautiful blue color of the water was caused by mercury used to mine the gold. The mercury made the fish dangerous to eat over a long period of time.

The group saw few other boats during the trip that afternoon as the shorelines of the jungle limned the distant horizon. Brazil nut trees towered above the other trees. After an appetizing on-board dinner prepared by the Brazilian chef from a four-star restaurant, most of the group were soon asleep even before darkness fell. Most were awakened by their arrival at 1:30 A.M. at the small village of Brasilia Legal where they would begin a new work. In the morning, they looked out on Av. Presidente (President's Avenue), a rather pretentious name for a long, narrow dirt street fronting the river. The town consisted of only two more dirt streets and everyone would have to wait until seven each night for four hours of electricity. Anyone making or receiving a telephone call would have to go to the village's only phone in the central office. Fortunately, the group had its own generator for electricity.

Pastor Eluardo, pastor at Itaituba but who worked with AMOR on the Tapajós River, greeted us early in the morning. As usual, he brought some from his church to aid in the work. The medical and dental teams set up in a small building, while the eyeglasses would be fitted in the city jail, vacant except for its caretaker. The owner of one of only two trucks in town volunteered his dilapidated pickup to carry the mahogany wood stored in the hold of the boat to the construction site.

Your author had heard some mention that he might be assigned to fit glasses, but since he received no instructions, he went along with the construction team. The Americans found that the foundation for the sanctuary had been laid in advance by Brazilians, but was larger than planned because it was built to fit the land space. Yours truly struggled to keep pace with the other workers, but as he was holding the hammer with both hands to drive his tenth 10-inch nail into the hard mahogany wood, Richard Walker informed him that he was to work as an "optometrist." With a sigh of relief, he headed for the jail house, but he had a feeling of satisfaction that he had nailed some planks for a church building that would remain termite-free forever. Although Richard called upon him for the nightly report of eyeglasses fitted, your author had relied heavily at first on Cristina Maltez, a Brazilian student from Ouachita Baptist University, since he knew little Portuguese. Helen Thompson kept the records and aided greatly in keeping things in order. Dr. Marvin Robertson, an Arkadelphia optometrist, had written the prescription for the eyeglasses on each envelope, so the supposed "optometrist" gradually became adept in selecting the proper pair on the first try. They fitted fifty-three that first day. They found out later that some people of the town had tried to prevent the jail from being used, but the caretaker had insisted, "These people are doing good and I *will* permit them to use the jail."

Winston fell down a flight of stairs in the boat. Since no X rays could be taken, it was not known whether he might have broken an ankle, leg, or foot. He was in agonizing pain, but a few days later, still taking antibiotics, he carried on his work of supervising the boat crew while hobbling around on crutches made by a member of the construction crew.

Randy Childs, a veteran construction worker, also toppled down the stairs the following day, but suffered only a sore arm. Jeff Bearden, another construction worker, was sidelined temporarily by a bee sting.

Wednesday, the second day at Brasilia Legal, was an eventful day as the medical crew dealt with an alcoholic who seemed to become demon-possessed at times. They then delivered a six-pound boy to an unwed sixteen-year-old girl at 6:00 P.M.

Pastor Daniel left on Thursday prepared to take a favorable report of the AMOR work to the Brazil Home Mission Board. He was especially impressed by the primitive conditions that the group endured while carrying on the work. Perhaps he had spied me at night crawling on my stomach under the hammocks to get to the bathroom at the opposite end of the boat. He might have been in the hammock I bumped as I failed to get low enough!

Daniel planned to talk to Mario Ikedo, director of evangelism for the state convention. The state executive secretary had told Daniel that he would like to cooperate with AMOR, but had to "be careful because of much pressure." He was referring to opposition from the Equatorial Brazil Mission. The Walkers could only ask, "Why, God? What have we done?" The cause for hostility remained a mystery to them.

The volunteers found that other opposition had preceded them. Four nuns had visited Brasilia Legal the week before they had arrived and had told the people not to listen to the Americans since what they said came from the Devil. The group's solicitude for their welfare, however, soon won the confidence of most of the townspeople. An attempt to organize a boycott against the group also failed.

In addition to keeping busy with the various tasks during the day, the group members found their nights were busy ones as they held nightly services in the sanctuary long before their activities were finished. Each member of the group gave his or her testimony, with Richard translating into Portuguese. Since your author had some mastery of Spanish and had listened to a tape in Portuguese for a year, he decided to give his in Portuguese. He read it twice to Maria, a helper from Aveiro, and she corrected some of his pronunciation. A number of Brazilians were kind enough to say that they understood every word he read. Daniel preached the first night, but Richard preached for most of the services. The Brazilians seemed to enjoy hearing the Americans singing in English and also repeated a simple chorus in Portuguese.

The group members' activities did not end with church services as they gathered in the boat each night for a report of the day's activities and a devotional before retiring for the night. Your author found that he could sleep better on the twelve-inch-wide bench than he could in the hammock. Helen Thompson, whose hammock was directly behind him, was greatly disturbed by his inability to sleep in the hammock. Her husband, Clarence, had no difficulty in dropping off to sleep immediately in a hammock.

The insomnia, however, allowed yours truly to stroll out on the deck and gaze in wonder and awe for the first time at the Southern Cross and other stars of the Southern Hemisphere gleaming in the clear sky. At night, the crew always pulled out into the river and enjoyed a cool but mosquito-free sleep. Your author awoke one morning to find a bat hanging above his head. Ken Ramsey, whose hammock was adjacent to mine, caught it in a gloved hand and released it. When it soon returned, he reluctantly killed it.

It amazed the Americans to see the sacrifices the Brazilians would make to seek medical help. One woman walked twenty-three kilometers, others paddled canoes for many hours, and all had to wait in line for hours in the hot sun before their needs could be met. One ninety-one-year-old man accompanied by his eighty-nine-year-old wife trekked eighteen kilometers through the jungle to see a doctor for the first time and could not understand why he was so exhausted. They had spent the night in the jungle. He was diagnosed as having a hernia, but immediately after treatment, they began their return voyage.

The volunteers did not feel guilty when they took off early Friday afternoon for swimming and sunbathing. Even though the men were experienced swimmers, some of them were surprised by the strong undertow. Some dived off the top of the boat. A Brazilian girl, Melinda Rhone, decided to swim, but when she felt the strong undertow, she quickly caught hold of the rope and pulled herself back into the boat. The Brazilians later said they had sighted alligators where the men had been swimming

Saturday, July 1, marked the first time in thirty-nine years that your author was not present to celebrate his son's birthday. It was the thirty-fourth wedding anniversary for Richard and Bea. She had always wanted a cruise, so they planned one that morning in a small boat to Fordlândia in the company of Pastor Eluardo and Raimundinho. Bea cancelled her part of the trip when one of the translators for the medical team became sick. After the boat devotional that night, the group surprised the couple with an anniversary cake cooked by Helen Thompson.

Bea started her Sunday morning early with vomiting and high fever. Three others on the boat also had fever. As usual, the Americans held their Sunday morning services on the boat. The group shared their experiences, then Richard preached on the work of the Holy Spirit.

That afternoon the Americans found out that Brazilians could play better soccer when the townspeople, along with the boat crew, beat their taller opponents in seven out of eight sets. Later, a large crowd gathered at the river's edge as Richard and Eluardo baptized ten, with four of them from Brasilia Legal, four from Barreiras, and two from Aveiro.

The final service Monday night was a victorious one, with an overflow crowd and three adults making decisions for Christ. The Americans stood in front of the pulpit as the congregation filed by to give them hugs and fond farewells.

Your author was the lone "optometrist" on Monday, the final day, as Cristina was helping the medical team and Helen was cooking a banana pudding. When the crowd made a mad rush to select their own glasses, he managed to get them back in line by shouting "No" several times in Portuguese. The work went smoothly and he had given out some forty eyeglasses before Helen arrived to help him, then she gave out the final 10 for a total of 61 that morning and a total of 294 for the five days of work.

The medical team closed its clinic at 10:00 A.M. on Tuesday and began to load its remaining supplies on the boat. It had seen 524 patients and extracted 979 teeth. The construction crew did some finishing touches on the church building before packing up its tools. Vacation Bible Schools had averaged 141 in attendance. A total of thirty-six decisions had been made in the homes and fifteen public decisions made in the services, with ten baptisms.

Clarence Thompson and your author strolled down a dirt road that had been constructed with the grandiose idea of linking the river town with a highway, but which was beginning to become overgrown with jungle vegetation. They ventured about fifty yards on a jungle trail but saw no animals or birds, which many people would expect. They did see a giant termite nest hanging from a tree.

As they prepared for departure, the Americans were greeted with a homemade sign in front of the boat saying, "Obrigado. Brasilia Legal agradece" (Thanks. Brasilia Legal Appreciates). Pastor Eluardo and wife, Maria dos Anjos, along with others who had worked with the Americans, came on board the *Livramento IV* to express their appreciation and to say farewell. It was quite an emotional experience. Eluardo gave each some Brazil nuts as a remembrance.

With fond farewells, the group pulled away from Brasilia Legal at noon. They stopped at Aveiro to inspect the sanctuary built by the previous group. Naturally, they thought their own construction crew had done a better job. They had to rush back to the boat when Richard realized that people would soon swamp the group with pleas for medical service. Clyde Tempel did set the broken arm of a young lad, who proudly displayed his sling to the other youngsters crowded around the boat.

When they reached Santarém, they continued until they crossed where the clear blue Tapajós merged with the sandy Amazon, then took a short ride on the Amazon before docking at Santarém. After a day of shopping in Santarém and an afternoon in Manaus, they left at 5:30 P.M. for Rio de Janeiro. Here your author visited with his missionary niece, Janis Sumerlin, who, surprisingly, had years before participated in the fifteenth birthday celebration of Cida Walker.

Rain dampened the visit to Rio, but most of the group preferred the Amazon to this dirty urban center with its homeless people huddled in cardboard boxes along the streets. All were glad to leave for home early Sunday morning.

The Brasilia Legal trip was important because many of the founders of AMOR were participants. It has been dealt with in detail, too, because of the author's involvement and because it would typify subsequent missions in scope and methods. Some later missions would be larger, some similar in scope, and some smaller. Almost all missions would build a standard-size church out of mahogany wood, or would construct a parsonage or additional educational space. Each would conduct a Vacation Bible School and nightly services. Most would offer medical, dental, and optometry services. Each of the trips would have unique aspects, however, so the most unusual and noteworthy of these will be chronicled.

Chapter 16

The Arkadelphians would soon be followed by the final two AMOR trips for 1989. Gracemont Baptist Church of Tulsa, Oklahoma, sent its second group for the period of July 24–31 to Estrada Oito, two miles from Belterra, one of two Brazilian towns built by Henry Ford before the manufacturer of synthetic rubber and more economical Malaysian rubber. Also making their second trip were Dr. and Mrs. Alan and Linda Winberry of Salem, Arkansas.

Docked five miles from Belterra and two and a half miles from the work site, the team had to depend upon Pastor João Carlos's old truck and the Walkers' friend Diorlando's pickup for transportation. These frequently proved less than dependable as the truck had to be pushed to get started and on its first return trip stopped dead a mile from the boat. The boat mechanic returned to clean the filter and drive the truck back.

Two noteworthy events occurred on Wednesday, July 26. Richard stopped to pick up a woman with three children, one of whom was ill. She told him, "Some foreigners are in Estrada Oito and I will find them upon arrival."

Richard shared his faith with her, prompting her to ask, "Are you a pastor?" He replied that he was and that he had brought the "foreigners." She exclaimed, "How about that! Here I am riding with the 'Chief'!"

In the clinic, a woman with tears streaking down her face, commented, "Everyone in the region knows you are here, and no one even knew to ask for you! No one ever comes here to help us. We are emotional and impressed that you would come."

After Richard told a tour administration group meeting what AMOR was doing, the directors begged for a similar team in Belterra. Meanwhile, back at the clinic, Mary Kirkland, the dental hygienist, who was hypoglycemic, hyperventilated and dehydrated at the same time. She lay unconscious on the floor for an hour while she was given an IV and breathed into a plastic bag.

Boyd made the eighty-minute round trip to get the needed IV fluids that were on the boat. Within fifteen minutes after receiving the fluids, she was responding. She was carried in the back of the pickup to the boat where four crewmen, with her IV still running, lifted her on board. Although still extremely weak, Mary was laughing and talking that night.

Three of the Walkers celebrated birthdays during the trip: Cida on July 27, Odemeia on July 28, and Bea on July 29. All three days were work days as usual. Forced to push the truck on Saturday, the undaunted group sang, "Heigh Ho! Heigh Ho! It's off to work we go . . . " That night Bea was treated to a surprise birthday party with a huge plastic rabbit made of Little Richard's balloons, and dessert of Brazilian "goodies" prepared by Odemia and Cida.

Little Richard was a delight, not only to his doting Walker grandparents, but to everyone on board as he became the boat's mascot.

Illness struck the group again on Sunday when David Barnes, the pharmacist, suffered a possible stroke while swimming. He was knocking into the other swimmers, his speech was slurred, his left eye and that side of his face drooped, and he could not squeeze with his left hand. His blood pressure was high. Boyd rushed to the clinic to get the needed medicine. By the time he returned eighty minutes later, the pharmacist had stabilized. A nurse, however, was beginning to dehydrate.

By Monday, July 31, the final day of the mission, the team was decimated by illness. The medical team limped through the morning as two nurses and the pharmacist remained on board the boat. Others did not go to work because of various sicknesses.

The people were desperate to get into the clinic before it closed at noon. One lady, carrying a baby, praised God loudly as she came through the door. She had been trying since Tuesday to get in, but had been shoved aside each time she had tried to get a number.

The missionary group endured the heat aboard the boat until time for the baptism of thirteen obedient Christians at the river's edge. Most of the 110 witnesses had walked the five miles from Belterra.

Bea was impressed that despite the suffocating heat and having to push the truck to get it started, the group had ridden cheerfully the mile and a half to work over nearly impassable roads with red dust blowing in their faces. Once they rode over a six-foot boa constrictor three times, but it managed to crawl away. None of the volunteers had complained or shown laziness. The team committed itself to returning to Belterra in 1990 to bring again the needed medical and evangelism team to serve the people.

The final group for 1989 arrived in Santarém on Monday, August 7, for the eight-hour boat ride to Monte Sião on the Arapiuns River, a tributary of the Tapajós, which is a tributary of the Amazon. The group of twenty-six were mainly from Vian (Oklahoma) Baptist Church, but some came from Florida and an eighty-year-old woman from Arkansas.

The medical team worked in a building, but glasses were fitted and Vacation Bible School was held in the heat under mango trees. A construction crew painted and repaired the small church. One of the team was a hairdresser and delighted those waiting in the medical line by cutting and combing many heads of hair, then putting berets and ribbons on their hair. Pastor Dan Caldwell delighted both young and old with his magic tricks.

This was a communal village of ten houses and about a hundred persons. If fish were caught or an animal killed, everyone ate. If nothing was caught, no one ate. Two hogs were killed during that week and the Americans were humbled when one-fourth was presented to them.

Visible results included 543 patients seen, 1,000 teeth extracted, 89 glasses given, and an average of 89 in attendance in VBS, 60 decisions made during personal witnessing and 16 in church, 10 baptisms, and the repair and repainting of the existing church building.

The volunteers committed themselves to return in 1991 to erect a new church and to bring a full medical and evangelistic team.

Workers, both experienced and inexperienced carpenters, are shown constructing a typical temple of termite-proof mahogany wood, one of many AMOR volunteers have built in the Amazon Basin.

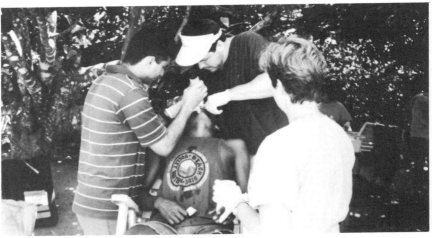

A dental team sets up an "office" under the shade of a mango tree to administer dental services.

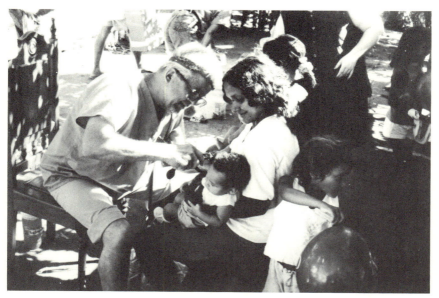

Another phase of the multi-purpose missions of Amazon Mission Organization is shown as a physician examines the ear of a tiny patient, while a child who has been treated walks away with her balloon.

A young volunteer has her hands full as she holds the attention of a large group of young children in Bible School. Sometimes as many as 1,300 attended Bible School and had to be divided into different sessions.

Chapter 17

The first AMOR trip in 1990 was the first conducted in cooperation with the Brazil Home Mission Board. Beginning on December 27, 1989, the trip to Aveiro extended until January 7 and included volunteers from Florida, Georgia, Arkansas, Oklahoma, and Kentucky. Bea acted as team leader since Richard had gone to Brazil on December 24 with Dr. Al Harvey and his eleven-year-old daughter Holly to see what medicine was already on hand and to purchase more.

She soon ran into many of the problems encountered by a group leader. She was told that the airline was cancelling eleven of the reservations from Miami because the persons holding these could not check in two hours before boarding. The travel agent assured her they would not be cancelled. Then Pan American cancelled its flight from Atlanta to Miami, but the travel agent switched the three stranded volunteers to Delta.

While waiting to leave Santarém for the ten-hour boat ride to Aveiro, Richard was interviewed by a local newspaper reporter who asked why the group was there. Richard told the reporter that many people of all ages were dying of a mysterious disease in Aveiro and cries for help had gone unheeded. The reporter took a picture of the group, and Bea prayed that God would use the publicity to His glory.

The twenty-one American volunteers on this trip were joined by three interpreters, two doctors, an electrician, and a pastor, sent by the Brazil Home Mission Board. These included also three crew members, three cooks, a young lady from Santarém, a couple from Minas Gerais, Richard, Bea, Boyd, and Winston with his family; the two rented boats were loaded.

As usual, the physicians, dentist, and Vacation Bible School leaders toiled relentlessly in the oppressive heat, with 450 children attending the final day of VBS. One young man with malaria and a temperature of 106 degrees came to the clinic, but responded well to intravenous treatment.

The construction crew discovered that it took more time to build a parsonage for Pastor Eduardo than to erect a temple, so that job was not quite completed. Services were held nightly in the sanctuary, with nine new converts baptized at dusk of the final day. A total of 676 medical patients were seen and 595 teeth extracted.

Bea wrote in her diary: "This first AMOR–Home Mission Board project has been exciting and highly blessed of God. We look forward to the remaining three trips of 1990. As it grows, and more people in Brazil learn of it, we would believe the HMB will be able to participate in all the AMOR trips."

This first trip of 1990 was to provide benchmarks in that it produced two significant events. Because of the lack of bathrooms, AMOR was forced to rent two boats for most of the trips. Such was the case on this trip as the volunteers were on the *Eutemio Seleski* and *The Anderson*. Winston and Boyd had rented these boats many times and once the owner had mentioned that he would like to sell one of these for the unreal price of $40,000. Richard knew that the motor alone, even in its present condition, was worth that price.

The Walkers had long felt the need for a boat owned by AMOR and the AMOR Board had voted approval back in October of their buying or building a boat in 1990. Richard contacted the owner of *Eutemio Seleski* and asked for fifteen days to raise the money. He then contacted Robbie Rudolph, board chairman, and he began the process of borrowing the money. The owner of the boat would doubtless later wonder many times why he had sold the boat at such a low price.

The Walkers gave credit to God that He had worked His will for their work. Long before the boat had been purchased, Richard, Winston, and Boyd had selected its name—*AMOR/Beatriz*. Bea was overwhelmed that they named it in her honor.

Approximately $15,000 was spent to make modifications to make it suitable for AMOR use. AMOR added three bathrooms and made other necessary changes. These additions were made possible by a gift from Jack and Mary Lea Taylor of Humble, Texas. On December 2, 1991, Dr. David Shuler, a board member from Joplin,

This launch was purchased by AMOR in October 1990 for $40,000 and was named *AMOR/Beatriz* by her family in honor of Bea Walker. AMOR added $15,000 in modifications to make it more suitable for its purposes.

Missouri, sent a check for $30,382.21 to pay off the remaining debt on *AMOR/Beatriz*. Several board members from Murray, Kentucky, had previously accepted the responsibility to pay the interest on the loan until it was paid in full.

The *Beatriz* was not a fast boat as compared to yachts in the United States. Powered by one 393-HP Scania diesel engine with a four-foot, three-bladed propeller, it traveled at approximately twelve miles per hour. It had a fuel capacity of 2,200 liters and consumed approximately 50 liters an hour. Two 7.5 KW generators on board were powered by an 11-HP, one-cylinder diesel engine and provided for 110 volts, 60 cycle energy at all times.

The boat was required by law to have a crew of four: a captain, a mechanic, and two deck hands. In addition, the Walkers hired a cook and two assistants for each trip, plus one crew member to help keep things clear and to wash the clothes of the team members. Two crew members had to be maintained at all times even when not traveling.

This was the second trip made to Aveiro where Baptist work was begun for the first time less than seven months ago. This important little town on the Tapajós River would later become the site of the AMOR hospital for the region.

Nine men from the First Baptist Church of Orlando, Florida, accompanied Richard to Santarém March 7–18 to build a temple and to conduct evangelistic services. Boyd and Winston had done the advance work at Santarém.

In addition to completing the temple, the volunteers rejoiced at the twenty-one new Christians they had helped to convert.

Richard was especially elated with the events of Friday night, March 9. He wrote:

> We invited the missionary family for supper tonight. They all came—Bobby Leonard with wife Donna, David, Cristy, and Ryan, plus the Journeyman, Robin. We praise God that they accepted our invitation. It really seems that God has broken down all the barriers. We were offered the use of whatever equipment he has; wants to leave us whatever medicines, eyeglasses, tools, etc., he has when he goes home on furlough. We really did have a great time of fellowship. I spent an hour and a half with Bobby earlier today, and noted this change. Tonight, the walls fell. Praise the Lord!

Richard thought his sons had forgotten his fifty-eighth birthday on March 10, but Winston and Boyd surprised him that night with filet mignon and cake.

Another *AMOR* experience was in store May 20–30 at Santa Cruz on the Tapajós River for twenty-seven volunteers from Florida, Tennessee, and Kentucky. As had other groups, they had undergone a year of preparation in planning, praying, and gathering supplies. In Brazil, on the other hand, Winston and Boyd had worked endless hours in the weeks preceding the trip by getting construction materials to the site and having two Brazilians lay the groundwork for the building. Winston and Boyd purchased 1,800 liters of mineral water for $800 to take on board the *AMOR/Beatriz* along with other supplies. They also secured interpreters and took care of countless other details.

The team would be on the newly purchased boat. Some remodeling had been done, but it was not completely refurnished. It had many conveniences already, however, that could not be found on the rented boats.

All tools and supplies, along with a generator, were carried to the work site by wheelbarrows. Santa Cruz had electricity only four hours at night. Despite working often in the rain in the chigger-infested grass in the poverty-stricken area of mostly mud-thatched huts, the team was able to accomplish marvelous things such as taking out two tumors, putting a cast on a three-year-old who broke her upper thigh bone, and fitting glasses on two persons who otherwise were totally blind. Bea was bitten by a snake as she walked through the grass to church, but the snake evidently was not very poisonous as the wound healed quickly.

In addition to starting a new work, the team completed a new thirty-by-sixty-foot church building of new mahogany wood, had eighty-five professions of faith with 15 baptisms, and had an average of 234 in Daily Vacation Bible School. The medical team saw 616 patients, extracted 589 teeth, and fitted 183 pairs of glasses.

Maria dos Anjos, wife of Pastor Eluardo Veloso, dedicated the following poem to the team (translated by Bea Walker):

I give thanks for this life that my God gave me,
I give thanks for this team that worked so much here.
Thanks for your strength that helps me so much.
Without measuring great distance, your work was so worthwhile.
I give thanks for this team, and for your decision to come here.
To God we render thanks, and pray He'll give you more
    protection.
May your lives always have much peace and much love.
May you always be used in the Lord's service.
This night there is much happiness because of the work and the
    fellowship.
There is one faith and only one strength between our two great
    nations.
Now we ask God not to let us walk alone,

But to let us take the message to the upper Tapajós River.

The Walkers would have a little more than a month before they would begin a frantic pace of sponsoring five AMOR trips within the next three months. Because of suffering from acute attacks of arthritis, however, Bea would not return to Brazil for two years. During this time, she did not get to see Little Richard, her grandson.

Team members from Florida, Arkansas, and Louisiana traveled to Santa Maria on the Uruará River for a tour of duty from July 4 to 15. This village of three thousand was only three hours from the Amazon and was the hometown of Odemeia, Winston's wife.

The work went smoothly, with Vacation Bible School attendance averaging 320. A total of 126 made professions of faith in door-to-door visitation and 74 in church services. The physicians saw 881 patients, and dentists extracted 1,035 teeth. The optometrist fitted 560 pairs of glasses.

How much was all of this worth at current prices in Santarém? A total of $61,600 in glasses were given away, and this did not include the cost of examination. The visits to the doctor would have cost $30,835, not including medicine. Add the cost of dental care and the construction of a new church building and one can get an idea of the contributions of this team to the village.

Winston and Boyd had only four days to prepare for the next group of volunteers. They came from the First Baptist Church of Albuquerque, New Mexico, to stay in Fordlândia from July 18 to 29. Cida Walker was the team leader this time as she met the group in Miami.

Americans had pulled out of Fordlândia in 1948 after real rubber was no longer profitable, but they had left behind a fully equipped hospital with no personnel or money. As a result, the AMOR medical team was able to use the hospital as a clinic for the first time in forty years.

Visiting this group to discuss the work of AMOR were Johnny Burnett, Orman Gwynn, and Bill Richardson, who came in the missionary plane along with missionary pilot Warren Rose, who also assisted at the hospital. Accompanying them were Pastor Oliveira de Araujo, executive secretary for the Brazilian Baptist Home Mission Board; Milton Macedo, executive secretary for Pará Baptist State Convention; and Pastor Eluardo, home missionary who always worked with AMOR.

Richard and Boyd, along with Dr. Joe McKinney and Rosie McPeak, AMOR board members, met with the group, who seemed favorably impressed with the work, which was a new one for Fordlândia and left behind a new church building.

Two separate works were run simultaneously from August 1 to 12 by First Southern Baptist Church of Del City, Oklahoma, and Gracemont Baptist Church of Tulsa, Oklahoma. Both groups traveled together to Santarém, where they were shuttled to the *AMOR/Beatriz* for breakfast. After remaining in Santarém until midafternoon, the Del City group of twenty-one plus interpreters departed on the boat for Terra Santa on the Nhamundá River, while the Gracemont group of twenty-seven plus interpreters boarded a bus for a bumpy one-and-a-half-hour ride to Belterra.

In addition to the medical, dental, and optometry work, the Del City team started a new work and built a new temple on this beautiful peninsula on the dark Nhamundá River. Gracemont volunteers were making their second trip to Belterra where the medical team saw 804 patients, the dental team extracted 624 teeth, the optical team fitted 227 pairs of glasses, Vacation Bible School averaged 265, 88 decisions were made, and 7 were baptized. A building was almost completed.

Volunteers from both teams were forced to sit up during one enforced all-night vigil at Manaus since officials would not allow anyone to lie down at the airport.

Dr. Patricia Garnett kept a journal of the last AMOR trip of 1990 to Maracana near Santarém from September 19–30. She was surprised that six adults would be sleeping in hammocks within her 8-by-10-foot area of the deck.

As she was in charge of Vacation Bible School along with four others, she told mainly of her experiences as a VBS leader. She was moved to tears the first day while preparing for the first class as she realized that she would no longer just be praying for missions, but would be actively communicating God's word. She had hoped for only 200 the first day so that she could get adjusted, but an estimated 425 showed up.

On the final day, the VBS leaders had 400 children in the morning, then took a short break for lunch. They loaded the van for the final trip that afternoon and were amazed to see more than 900 persons waiting for them. The leaders gave out 750 coloring books and 75 boxes of crayons before their supply was exhausted.

The church, completed except for one panel and the doors, was filled to overflowing for the final night service, which ended in hugs of farewell for the volunteers from Coral Baptist Church of Coral Springs, Florida.

Chapter 18

As the last 1990 AMOR trip was completed on September 30, the Walkers had three months to make additional modifications on the *Beatriz*. Even before the $15,000 in improvements had been completed, AMOR had seen the value of owning its own boat as it now had many of the conveniences missing on a rented boat. No longer did trips have to be planned around the times the boats would be available for renting.

Despite all of the preparations, however, the first trip of 1991 from January 9 to 20 did not start smoothly. When the engine overheated in a trial run, a mechanic had to repair it by unclogging the water for the cooling system of the heat exchanger. Then it was discovered that all three batteries aboard the boat were dead and needed a quick charge. A short in the voltage regulator was draining the power from the batteries, so a trickle charger was purchased and the batteries were used only to start the engine. All running lights and the spotlight were tied to 110 volts from the generator.

The January group of volunteers from Arkansas, Missouri, and Oklahoma comprised a medical/dental team, which traveled to Jurutí, Curumucury, and Santa Rita. The medical team dealt with some unusual cases. After they had treated a man with a snake bite, he stood around for quite a while. Meanwhile, a woman standing near the dental clinic told Richard in dead seriousness that she was waiting to go to the medical clinic to put her name into the "pot," but that she could not go over there until the snake man left. She was pregnant and said if she looked at a snake-bitten man, her baby would vomit a lot and would be lame at the spot where the man was snake-bitten!

The doctors saw a case of elephantiasis on a young man's right foot and also lanced a large abscess on a young boy's upper right thigh. They also diagnosed two children with chagas, a fatal disease caused by the Barbados bug.

The dental team had a number of patients with abscesses already perforating the jaw. For some unknown reason, patients in the area bled rather profusely.

The lasting impact made by previous groups in 1986 and 1988 was seen when the team visited the little church in the lake of Curumú-Curí. Katia, the daughter of community leader Vivaldo, had been retarded since birth and talked only a little, but she remembered a young college student, Camille (Davis in 1986), who had sung "Amazing Grace." Katia sang with much enthusiasm the exact same tune, but with sounds all her own—neither English nor Portuguese.

The medical team was exhausted after seeing more than 1,400 patients. It had run out of aspirin, Tylenol, and worm medicine. The dental team, also very tired, had seen 411 persons and had extracted 696 teeth.

In addition, eleven professions of faith were made during the trip. Twelve who had been waiting a year for an ordained pastor were baptized. Richard explained that it did not take an ordained minister to baptize or hold the Lord's Supper.

Dr. and Mrs. Ken Turner were the leaders of a team from Joplin, Missouri, to São Luiz on the Tapajós River from May 15 to 26.

Richard Walker summed up the trip: "There has been a fruitful harvest this week. We must leave São Luiz, but only physically. This dedicated team of volunteers will never again be the same. They leave a part of themselves here in this far-away village—abandoned by the world, but not by God Almighty."

Visible results showed in 100 professions of faith, 11 baptisms, 1,198 medical patients treated, 468 teeth extracted, 120 pairs of eyeglasses fitted, an average of 279 attendance in Vacation Bible School, a new work begun, and a church building completed.

"Grandma" Chris Barr of DeWitt, Arkansas, recorded the trip of June 12 to 26 to the village of Prainha on the banks of the Amazon approximately eight hours by boat from Santarém by a team from the First Baptist Church of Russellville, plus others from northwest Arkansas, Oklahoma, and Louisiana. The Walkers, at the request of the Brazilian Home Mission Board, made plans for this and subsequent trips a year in advance.

Dr. Jim Carter of Russellville and his medical team were the busiest as patients began coming to the boat early in the morning. Winston Walker found a building for them to work in, but in the afternoon they worked under the shade of a tree because of the heat. In all, they saw 1,420 patients, while the dental team extracted 452 teeth and the optical team fitted 177 pairs of eyeglasses. A total of 2,301 children attended Vacation Bible School. A total of 234 decisions were made and 5 persons were baptized. A church building was completed and a new work was begun.

Dan Shipley led and Pediatric Nurse Practitioner Faye Austin recorded the trip sponsored by the First Baptist Church of Murray, Kentucky, to Lago Sapacuá from June 30 to July 10.

Unlike other volunteers who had seen few animals and birds along the fringes of the jungles, Faye and three others were taken by a guide for an early-morning boat ride into the jungle. Here they saw kingfishers, hawks, red-capped cardinals, parrots, and herons, along with marshes, grass resembling Johnson grass floating on the water, lily pads, annatto trees with hanging red pods, as well as banana, papaya, palm, and Brazil nut trees.

Large termite bags hung on many of the trees, and other trees had huge bromeliads of the orchid family living as parasites on them. They observed many large iguanas in the trees and a big tarantula half out of its web.

The team built a new temple and began a new work with 38 professions of faith and 34 baptisms, along with an average attendance of 122 in Vacation Bible School. The medical team treated 870 patients, the dental team extracted 576 teeth, and 226 pairs of eyeglasses were fitted.

For the fourth consecutive year, Gracemont Baptist Church of Tulsa, Oklahoma, sponsored a trip to Brazil, this time to Fordlândia on the Tapajós River from August 4 to 14. Team members, however, also came from New Mexico, Arkansas, Tennessee, and Texas.

The trip began with what Richard Walker termed two miracles. The first occurred when the group's baggage arrived in Manaus in relatively good condition despite the fact that an accommodating Delta Airline manager had committed a "no-no" and checked a number of their pieces of equipment directly through to Brazil. The other miracle occurred when a Varig representative said that the customs officials had asked him to lead the group through. The officials had already left the area.

A Santarém television station had heard about the equipment AMOR had shipped in for the hospital, so a crew was waiting at Winston's home to film and interview the team. Odemeia, Winston's wife, saw the television special that night and said it was excellent.

Because of the well-equipped but no-longer-used hospital that the Americans had left behind when Ford abandoned its rubber industry in 1948, the medical team was able to accomplish more than any previous group, even performing a record three surgeries in one day. Each physician was able to have his own room and a separate room for dispensing drugs.

Thursday, August 4, began early for the electricians as they started to work in the attic of the hospital before the summer heat hit. Much electrical work had been done on the hospital, but much still remained to be done. The medical, dental, and optometry service began at 7:00 A.M.

If the tired team thought it would get a full night of rest, it was in for a rude awakening as a dental patient who was bleeding came to the boat at 2:00 A.M. on Friday. Then at 4:00 A.M. a Jeep came up and a man said a woman was about to give birth to a child. It turned out that she had already given birth, but had taken an overdose of pills after a spat with her husband. She was transported to the hospital and calm was restored to the boat until 5:30 A.M.

A huge crowd was waiting for the clinic to open Friday morning. Boyd had found an almost unbelievable number of patients in line when he went to the hospital at 4:00 A.M. None of the Americans were able to attend the evening worship service since they toiled on at the clinic until 9:00 P.M. Dr. Waldemar Lopez, a Brazilian, worked alongside the Americans, but never kept records of the number he treated.

Although an announcement was made Saturday that the clinic would be closed Sunday, a large number, many of whom had walked as long as twelve hours through the jungle or had traveled for several days, were begging to be treated.

Richard wrote:

One man came yesterday with his "backpack" full of bananas and other fruits for us. He came last year the same way. When someone told him to keep it for his family, he said, "We have enough."
   That really came home to us who have so much and many times want more. He was proudly wearing the trousers we gave him last year. If only some way I could get so many who have so much to just share a little with these who have nothing.
   NO ONE serves these people. No government. No church. No benevolent institution. None but AMOR comes to help the people unconditionally. If you are reading this and have a lot laid up for tomorrow, and more than you can use today, could you give some to help these who have such great needs TODAY?

In all, the medical team treated 1,252 in addition to Dr. Waldemar's patients and performed 30 surgeries, many more than ever before. The dental team extracted 519 teeth and the optometry team fitted 256 pairs of glasses. Six professions of faith were made and an average of 269 attended Daily Vacation Bible School.
   The last trip of 1991 would follow in only four days with Prestonwood Baptist Church of Dallas sponsoring a mission trip to Lago Mamaurú from August 18 to 28. No journals were shared with AMOR on medical and optometry work, but Curt Welwood wrote a journal on construction, Molly Hoebeke on Vacation Bible School, and Debra Montgomery on dental work.
   Winston had to return to Santarém after only a few days because his son was quite ill. John the Baptist, a Brazilian, and his sons, all carpenters, aided in the construction of the new temple so that it was finished on schedule.
   After the first day of Vacation Bible School, Molly Hoebeke wrote: "We returned to the boat. I did what I never dreamed I would do—jumped into the Amazon for a bath and head washing! All of these people have worms and many have lice, so, today I had two baths! I look pretty earthy—wild wavy hair, slicky skin, and the happiest heart and most peaceful spirit I have ever known! Thank you, Lord, for the opportunity to walk where You walked today! We had 48 kids this first day at VBS."
   The dental team consisted of two dentists, a dental assistant, a

dental hygienist, and an interpreter. They planned to work under a tree, but had no table. Four lads from the village eagerly constructed a table in only twenty minutes.

In addition to extracting 790 teeth, the team distributed toothbrushes and the interpreter instructed listeners on their use. There were few complications and only one mild post-operative infection. The medical team did not keep a journal, but treated 1,500 patients.

Seventy professions of faith were made and thirty-four were baptized.

Although this would be the final AMOR mission trip of 1991, an important new work would be initiated when the First Laymen's Institute or River Bank Bible Institute was held from November 11 to 23.

Since its inception in 1988, AMOR had never had an institute to train its lay church leaders. When a new work had been started and a temple had been built in a village, AMOR had only a short time to seek out lay persons who could take over the church leadership roles. Most of these did not even have a regular pastor, but had to depend upon irregular visits by a regional pastor. For instance, Eluardo Veloso served as the regular pastor in Aveiro, but also ministered to other churches established in villages along the Tapajós River.

Richard Walker was so eager to bring enough instructional material for the first training institute that he had to pay $150 to Varig for excess baggage. Bea had spent many hours typing and putting together studies of the Book of Hebrews, one entitled "Basic Doctrines of the Church" and the other on "Gifts of the Holy Spirit."

Richard had discarded his original intention of studying Religious Education and Church Polity because the pastors wanted to maintain control of the missions and would not let them develop on their own, "warts and all." Contrary to Richard's interpretation of the Scriptures, they were insistent on not allowing the workers to serve the Lord's Supper or to baptize. Instead of searching the Scriptures, the pastors would fall back on their "culture."

Before beginning the boat trip up the Tapajós River, Richard preached at Aldeia Baptist Church where he had pastored in Santarém and was humbled to find out that a Royal Ambassador chapter had been named in his honor. He was presented with one of their

T-shirts with EMBAIXADA RICHARD WALKER in large letters on the back. A translation of the presentation follows: "Dear Pastor Ricardo. We have chosen your name for our chapter because of all you represent in evangelism and for your life of dedication and work for the cause of Christ here. Because of this, we are proud to call our chapter 'RICARDO WALKER.' We offer this shirt of our chapter as a souvenir to you."

Richard had bought three books for each of those participating, along with a Portuguese hymnbook for each. Prestonwood Baptist Church of Dallas provided an inexpensive watch for each, while the First Baptist Church of Calico Rock, Arkansas, had sent along a hundred caps.

After all of the preparation on his part, he was disappointed to find that the men had done no advance study in preparation for the institute, but he was pleased with the thirty-one participants from fifteen different churches and their eagerness to learn. All slept and ate aboard the *AMOR/Beatriz*.

Richard wrote:

> Not one of these men studying with us is anywhere near fat. They are all trim and neat. Their clothes are hand-made. Most have only flip-flops for their feet. They've eaten better with us than ever before. The atmosphere is one of genuine joy, spiritual depth and happiness. Lots of laughing and fun at each other's expense. Fellowship of the genuine Christian kind. The guy I caught in the kitchen breaking his fast has been ribbed pretty hard. All are enjoying themselves.

Halfway through the second week, Richard perceived some answers to prayer and fasting when Pastor Eluardo of Aveiro announced that he was authorizing his lay leaders to baptize and to celebrate the Lord's Supper.

The participants expressed a need for having such an institute twice a year. Richard felt that he should restrict the number from each church to two in order to make it financially feasible.

Two of the participants would preach during the night services, then undergo critiques the next morning. The first three days were spent at Brasilia Legal, where the work was very weak. The group then moved on to Fordlândia where Richard noted that the congregation had become much more reverent than when he was last there. From Fordlândia the institute moved to Santa Cruz.

All of the participants expressed in writing their appreciation for the study. As translated by Richard, Josías dos Santos Pereira wrote:

> I'm very happy to be able to communicate with you, and through this letter I want to speak of the importance of your work and dedication and your involvement in the cause of evangelism. The Institute was exactly what we needed. We learned so much more than I knew in respect to what we studied, and only with the power of God can we acquire the knowledge needed to grow to be good leaders. Even though you aren't with us here, Dona Beatriz, we feel your presence with us, in the material you prepared for our study and in your husband being here. I would like you to know that I pray for you and thank you for all you do and that God will bless you richly.

A record number of 7,940 patients had been treated during the seven 1991 trips and five new works begun with five new temples constructed. In addition, 3,501 teeth had been extracted and 1,291 pairs of glasses fitted. A total of 445 professions of faith had been made with 96 baptisms performed. An average of 192 attended Vacation Bible School.

An important new work, the River Bank Bible Institute, had been started to train lay pastors.

Chapter 19

The AMOR team had been busy during the four months between the first Riverbank Bible Institute in November 1991, and its first 1992 trip to Nhamundá from March 13 to 23. In Brazil Winston was completing the painting of the *Beatriz*, while the AMOR Board of Directors met in early March at DeGray Lake Resort near Arkadelphia, Arkansas, in a prayer retreat.

It was at this retreat that the directors decided that it was the Lord's will that AMOR build a hospital in Aveiro to provide a medical ministry. At this meeting, one of the board members, Ron Carter of Dallas, offered to give $50,000 for the construction of the hospital. In addition to supplying the funds for the materials, Ron and his father, Don Carter of Dallas, organized a team of their own employees and took them to Aveiro in September to complete most the major structure of the hospital.

The hospital was a dream of those who had ministered in the Tapajós River area, since there was no medical help from Santarém to Itaituba, a distance of approximately 250 miles. AMOR at first offered to take from the Brazilian government the hospital built and then abandoned by Henry Ford at Fordlândia. AMOR wanted a ten-year lease with no strings attached, but the government offered it for only five years and attached too many restrictions.

After the prayer retreat at DeGray, Richard left for Brazil where he and Winston took the *Beatriz* out for water only to have the controls freeze. They bought a new accelerator and gear box, the only ones in Santarém, for $506. Eluardo Veloso told Richard that everything was ready for the second Riverbank Bible Institute in April.

The team of twelve left Santarém early on Saturday, March 14, and picked up missionary Ron Matthews and a lay worker, Aluízio, at Óbidos. Families had moved out of two houses at Nhamundá so that the medical team could work. A cool breeze greeted the team on the boat and the predicted mosquitoes failed to appear.

Some of the team laid out heavy timber, while others constructed benches and a pulpit for Sunday night services. Only a few came to see the medical team that afternoon, but a large crowd turned out for the services.

By Wednesday, many patients were coming to the clinic. On Wednesday, seventeen boats—not canoes—came with large groups of people and kept the medical team and dentist extremely busy. Despite all the crowds, the medical team was able to close its clinic Friday after attending to everyone—a first for AMOR.

The Lord blessed the team with 14 professions of faith, an average of 92 attendees in Vacation Bible School, 1,026 patients seen by the doctors, 500 teeth extracted, and 389 pairs of glasses fitted. The team completed a beautiful building and dedicated it on Friday night before leaving on Saturday.

The Second River Bank Bible Institute attracted a total of forty-two lay pastors and workers from April 3 to 20. This time Richard had more assistance, as Dr. John Wood of Waco, Texas, and Pastor Eluardo Veloso of Aveiro also served as professors. The institute began at Campo Alegre off Rio Cuminá, then moved to Mamaurú, then Lago Castanhanduba, Cuparí (above Aveiro), and finally Tumbira. The group chose as its theme song *"Segura Na Mao de Deus e Vai"* ("Hold God's Hand, and Go!").

Richard had opportunity to visit with Winston and Boyd during the trip. Winston had been having severe shortness of breath and had hyperventilated twice. He saw Dr. Russ Howard on April 21 and found that his problems were caused by stress.

While at Aveiro, Richard found out that Mr. Mixo, the owner of some beautiful river-front property suitable for the building of a hospital, would deal only with him. Richard was able to make a deal without very much trouble as Mr. Mixo was being pressured by people elated at the prospect of a hospital.

Thirteen of those participating in the institute were new, while the others had attended last November. Ageu Veloso of Itaituba epitomized the general feeling of the participants: "This study has been a fountain of spiritual water from which you drink. I have learned more from these studies than I have learned during all the rest of my life. Because of this, I ask that you who have invested in this Institute never to think that your investment has been in vain, because we have all learned much."

After toiling for AMOR in the States but being prevented from making the mission trips because of arthritis, Bea returned to Brazil for the first time in two years by accompanying Richard and a group of twenty. Of this group from the Harmony Heights Baptist Church of Joplin, Missouri, most had made the trip to São Luiz the previous year, but some were on their first trip to Brazil. They would work from May 8 to 18 at Tumbira in a village just off the Tapajós River. Bea recorded the trip.

Winston's wife, Odemeia, and Little Richard met them at the plane in Santarém. Bea wrote: "They were beautiful for my eyes to behold. Little Richard has grown tall and thin but his little face remains the same—very, very beautiful."

Bea aided the medical clinic as it saw 925 patients and filled 2,421 prescriptions. In fact, she was pampered so much by the boat crew, who brought her squeezed juice and various treats, that she was glad that the trip was for only ten days or she might have had to waddle off the boat! Working alone, the dentist extracted 402 teeth, while the optometrist fitted 175 pairs of eyeglasses. A total of 10 decisions were made and 34 were baptized. Little Richard was among the 521 attending Vacation Bible School.

None of the team of twenty missed more than a half day because of illness, and a majority of the group was talking about returning to the Amazon next year. Despite a late start, the construction team was able to complete a beautiful church building.

Neither Richard nor Bea accompanied the team from Arkansas, Oklahoma, and Texas that went to Santa Maria on the Uruará River for a stay from June 5 to 14, but Winston and Boyd had the boat ready at Santarém. Rosie McPeak, who had taken chemotherapy for cancer five years ago but was now cancer-free, recorded the trip.

The pastor for the week was the Rev. John Hodges of Viola, Arkansas. The team members must have done much personal witnessing as there were 233 professions of faith and 5 were baptized. A home was completed for the pastor and an average of 295 attended Vacation Bible School. The medical team saw 1,418 patients and gave out 2,169 prescriptions. A total of 317 teeth were extracted and 212 pairs of eyeglasses fitted.

Rosie concluded: "I still stand amazed with the work of AMOR—how *God and God alone* can take a person—a group of people—and work His great plan through them."

Despite approval by Brazilian officials in the United States for the July 3 to 13 trip to Aveiro by the First Baptist Church of Albuquerque, six boxes of medicines and most of the eyeglasses were detained by customs despite Richard's three hours of beseeching. God turned it into a blessing, however, since there was enough medicine for this trip and the medicine was sorely needed for the August trip.

In addition, Richard's brother Andy had a contact through Foster-Grant, a maker of glasses, and the company later sent 400 free glasses and another 400 at only $1.20 each. The detained medicine and eyeglasses were delivered to AMOR later in the week.

The Amazonas Baptist State Convention, with headquarters in Manaus, again approached AMOR about helping it expand its work in the interior of that state. Richard planned to take it up with the AMOR board of director in its meeting in Memphis on September 25 to 27.

A total of 50 professions of faith, 48 in the homes and two in the services, were made, 18 were baptized, an average of 213 attended Vacation Bible School and 2 prayer gazebos were completed. The medical team saw 1,150 and filled 2,926 prescriptions, while 73 pairs of were fitted. The medical team bemoaned cases that could have been prevented had the hospital in Aveiro been operational.

Nancy Welwood, one of seven veterans who had gone with the Prestonwood Baptist Church of Dallas to Mamaurú previously, recorded the trip by Prestonwood to Castanhanduba from July 17 to 28. Boyd Walker met the group in Belém, where officials kept the team members from sleeping during the long night in the airport. A newly clean-shaven Winston met the group in Santarém.

The seven veterans were overjoyed at passing by the church they had helped to construct and received a promise from Boyd to return. In fact, the group did switch from time to time from Castanhunduba to Mamaurú and conducted church services at both places. As a result, 28 were baptized at Mamaurú and 23 at Castanhunduba.

A new temple was constructed at Castanhanduba. Vacation Bible School, held in the Catholic church, attracted a total of 723. The medical team treated 901 patients, the dental team extracted 450 teeth, and the optometrist fitted 401 pairs of glasses.

The last group of volunteers for 1992 traveled to Brasilia Legal, staying from August 7 to 17. Richard became irritated by having to wait in line with his group of eighteen while others boarded U.S. Air at Miami only to find that his group was being assigned to Executive Class! Here they were served four-course meals on real china, given excellent service, and had large seats with plenty of leg room. He felt humbled by his impatience and God's providence.

The first AMOR work had begun in Brasilia Legal in the summer of 1989. Since that time Richard had found the village a difficult place for evangelism. This time, however, there were 255 professions of faith and 5 baptisms. Along with 450 teeth extracted and 502 pairs eyeglasses fitted, Richard's four-year dream was realized when, for the first time, 79 eye surgeries as well as four other surgeries were performed. The patients were excited at the prospect of having the eyesight to read again, to sew, or to mend fishing nets. Three lepers were among the 1,420 medical patients seen.

AMOR held its third 1992 River Bank Bible Institute from October 11 to 24 at Santa Maria on the Uruará River and at São Pedro and San Francisco on the Arapiuns River, a tributary of the Tapajós River. They started by towing a smaller boat, belonging to the boat boy, out on the rough Amazon, but the one-inch nylon rope soon broke. After three passes, the crew managed to rescue it from in front of an oncoming tow. Then the crew had to repair a broken steering wheel before retrieving the smaller boat.

The *Beatriz* was unable to come close to shore at most of their stops, so the jon boat had to make eight trips to carry everyone ashore. The *Beatriz* anchored a fourth of a mile offshore at Santa Maria, the first stop. Here three men preached a sermon each, but the large crowds seemed to enjoy the long services. So eager were all the participants to begin their Bible studies that Richard found himself unable to sleep past 5:30 A.M.

Then he arose at 4:00 A.M. to give some fishermen on the boat an early start! The fishermen, however, had no success until their guide showed them how to spear some of the large ones they couldn't otherwise catch.

Despite being deep in the jungle, Richard was able to talk with Bea twice on the one telephone available. Fortunately, it was hooked up to the rest of the world by satellite.

After discovering that most of the male adults in São Pedro were drunk after a drinking contest with a case of beer as the prize, the group passed up a night service and anchored offshore. The next day Richard picked out a prospective place for a worship service, but it belonged to the Catholic church and the group was told to leave. The volunteers sang and preached the gospel as they made their way back to the *Beatriz*.

The villagers did not come to the services, but peeped out from behind trees, while others listened from their small houses. Only a few children came up close. At the end of the service, the man who had ordered the group off the Catholic premises came up and requested one of the gold caps Richard had given each of the participants. This seemed to break the ice and others approached. The men gave up their caps, but they prayed that God had touched someone in the village.

After moving on from São Pedro, the group was able to anchor on the beach in front of the village of San Francisco. Here the team held services before a crowd of at least sixty villagers. Raimundinho, one of the participants, planned to spend half of his time on this river. He would begin at the mouth of the river and place New Testaments in each home.

Chapter 20

The year 1993 was a quite difficult one for AMOR. Since Varig, the Brazilian airline, kept changing its flight schedules, advanced scheduling became more complicated and some trips were made with less than a full boatload. As a result, AMOR Board members and other sources had to make up the difference in finances.

In mid-year, Winston moved to Manaus with his wife, Odemeia, son Richard and daughter Patricia, to earn his income by beginning "Fishing Adventures" and "Fish and Faith." He continued, however, to work as a volunteer for AMOR as an interpreter or in other capacities. Varig, meanwhile, firmed up its schedule at the end of 1993 so that the 1994 trips could be better planned.

It suddenly hit Richard when he arrived in Santarém for the River Bank Bible Institute to be held from February 20 to March 6 that for the first time since AMOR had started, neither of his two sons was there to meet him and have everything in readiness for the trip. They were both in the States with their families. Marcos Rego, who had been hired to manage the AMOR operations in Santarém, had done a superb job, however, and had everything almost ready for the Institute.

The *AMOR/Beatriz* had been repainted, had a new propeller, and its drive shaft had been newly aligned. After about five hours upriver, however, the fuel line clogged up and the boat drifted back down river while the line was unclogged. Thirty-five participants, with hopes of some more later, were on board as the group headed for Óbidos, where the first study would be done.

The River Bank Bible Institute went well, with the individuals eager to learn and readily speaking out on any problems they were having. After three days at Óbidos, the group left Wednesday night for Sapacuá for one day, then on Friday morning moved on to Jurutí, a small village on the banks of the Amazon River.

On the way, Richard talked to Pastor Eluardo about the fact that one of the young men was having trouble entering into the studies. Earlier, two men had told Richard that the young man was homosexual, but since Richard had no proof, he had admitted him when he requested to study with the group. Pastor Eluardo and two others, however, did have proof and confronted the young man. When they were unable to get him to agree to change his lifestyle, they had him leave the boat that day.

After the young man left, Richard, who along with several others had a touch of the flu, began to have so much pain that he was unable to leave his bed. He called Eluardo and some others and expressed his belief that he and some others who also suffered intense pain were being attacked by demonic activity.

They prayed together and rebuked the devil in Jesus' name. Immediately, the severe pain left Richard and the others who were suffering. The group fasted and held prayer meetings in all parts of the boat. Although they continued to have the flu, none of them suffered from the severe pains any longer.

Richard cautioned the participants that not every ache was caused by demonic activity. Since Richard could not seem to teach them not to put their drinking cups back among those not used, each soon suffered from the illnesses of others.

The church at Jurutí had called a full-time pastor for the first time in its sixty-six-year history. Pastor Rosinaldo had served without pay while encouraging the members to put all their resources into building a parsonage near the church. The parsonage AMOR had built earlier in the middle of town was being used as a school, with more than a hundred in attendance, so the members did not want to discontinue that use.

Richard concluded:

> The evangelistic zeal of these workers is a beautiful thing to behold. Eleven (11) of the works are absolutely on fire for our Lord. The Tapajós River area is an example. Their itinerant evangelist Raimundinho and Pastor Abiezer have really given good leadership.
>
> They have 50 men teaching other men basic doctrine and leading them to Jesus. They plan on training 200 such teachers this year. Last year their goal was 150 baptisms. They baptized 152. This year their goal is to win 1,500 to Christ and baptize 500. I believe they will do just that. PTL (Praise the Lord).

Richard was already looking forward to the next institute in the fall and to the dedication of the hospital at Aveiro during the annual Associational Meeting in July at Aveiro. People of the area had already promised to donate two steers, several pigs, chickens, sacks of rice, beans, and farinha for the occasion.

Boyd Walker led a group from the First Baptist Church of Orlando, Florida, to Lago de Jurutí Velho from March 20–30. The team departed from Santarém for Jurutí Velho at 4:45 A.M. Monday, March 22, and arrived at its destination, a beautiful site on the lake, at 2:00 P.M. Despite the late start, the construction team laid 25 percent of the floor for a new temple and the clinic was set up at a local gasoline station that day.

Despite storms, shortage of materials, and having to make some repairs to the *Beatriz,* the team made good progress. Boyd persuaded the public school teacher to suspend her classes for the week so that the students could attend the Vacation Bible School. The medical team delivered a 3.6 kilogram baby during the first morning of operation, while Boyd one night used a mounted flashlight as he extracted eleven teeth.

Overall, the team remained healthy despite some touches of flu. More than 1,600 medical patients were seen, Vacation Bible School averaged 217, a total of 17 made decisions, a temple was completed, and a new work begun.

The next trip from April 15 to 22 to Óbidos, sponsored by Twin Lakes Baptist Church of Mountain Home, Arkansas, was Richard's busiest and perhaps most rewarding one. In fact, he was so busy that he did not have time to write anything in his trip journal until April 20.

With letters from the mayor and director of the hospital of Óbidos inviting AMOR to come, the group had little trouble with the airport officials in Miami and Manaus. Winston, Odemeia, and grandchildren, Richard and Patricia, traveled from Santarém with the group.

Earl Hagar, an investment broker at Mountain Home, was trained by his dentist to anesthetize and pull teeth, but the team was without a regular dentist. Richard looked for a dentist who could be hired for five days and found one with an office close to the AMOR clinic. He not only provided excellent service, but accepted Christ as his Savior in a night service during which Earl Hagar preached. Richard prayed that Wladimir, the dentist, would be the man God had raised up to lead the work at Óbidos.

The Vacation Bible School workers wondered whether anyone would show up the first day since the time had not been announced. Some 300 did show up, then the number arose to 750 the next session. The instructors decided to divide the group for the next day, with the boys coming in the morning and the girls in the afternoon. A total of 400 boys attended the next morning, while 350 girls showed up for the afternoon. Then a total of 1,700 attended the final day!

In addition to fitting 404 pairs of eyeglasses, Dr. Doug Marx, the opthamologist, removed some 20 pterygiums plus performing other surgeries, such as removal of cysts and cataracts. At the request of his parents and with permission of his doctor, the AMOR team saw an eight-month-old boy who was dying despite being fed by IV. The Americans suggested mixing antibiotics, not available to the local doctor, with the IV. and the child improved greatly overnight.

The medical team saw a total of 1,340 patients, performed 30 surgeries, and gave out 2,500 prescriptions. The dentist extracted 375 teeth. The church building was repainted, and 48 made professions of faith by name, with many more in Vacation Bible School indicating their trust in Christ.

Various complications hit the trip led by Boyd to Maicurú, Paracary, and Jacaré Capá from June 18 to 29. After arriving in Belém, he discovered that eight boxes containing 90 percent of the medicines had never left Miami. Varig Airlines investigated and the supplies did arrive, but two days late.

Even before receiving word concerning the medicines, the group decided to push on to location at Jacaré-Pará to use what supplies it had. Work was going well in all areas, but Boyd learned that a fast-dropping water level, then only three feet below the keel in the secondary channel, was endangering the exit of the *Beatriz*. The channel by which they had come in was already closed. Having accomplished most of the projected tasks at Jacará-Pará, he decided to move to Paracary.

As the medical team prepared to pack its supplies, a man with a gunshot wound came in at 8:00 A.M. He had been shot in the arm and abdomen at 6:30 A.M. after an all-night party. Since his stomach was swelling and hardening from internal bleeding, it was decided to load him aboard the *Sabrina* along with a nurse and local sheriff and rush him to a Santarém hospital.

Thinking he was on his deathbed at the clinic, the wounded man called for his ten-year-old son and made him swear to avenge what had happened. Boyd knew that the man had thought about attending night church services, but had chosen instead to attend the party.

Boyd lamented: "End result: two families destroyed; one child haunted by his father's words, and all because of a party that took the place of receiving the gospel message. We of AMOR have much to do and many to reach."

Concerning his feelings after arrival at the next location, Boyd wrote: "It is really an odd feeling being here in Paracary again after 7 years. This was the first place that we ever did a full multi-ministry trip. It seems like it was only last month that the Arkadelphia (Arkansas) group was anchored out here on the lake aboard the *Viageiro III*. Boy, that was the trip that literally altered the entire course of my life. . . . Thank you, Lord!"

Among the 70 decisions for Christ was that of a team member, David Williams, who was baptized by Pastor John Hodges. In addition, an average of 203 attended Vacation Bible School, a church building and a home were repaired, 1,635 medical patients seen, 335 teeth extracted, and 596 pairs of eyeglasses fitted.

The First Baptist Church of Russellville, Arkansas, sponsored the trip to Jurutí and Oriximiná from July 2 to 13. Despite as many as 1,306 one day in Vacation Bible School and huge crowds attending night services in the park and the final one inside the church building, no professions of faith were made at Jurutí.

Richard felt the strong influence of Satan and read about a Satanic cult that, as part of their rites, had killed seven young boys and had castrated another who had escaped in Jurutí.

The medical team was kept busy at Jurutí in treating many

desperately sick people, including a man with a gangrenous leg, which was improving when they left. By Friday, there was no rush to open the clinic since most of the medicine on hand had been dispensed.

The team left Jurutí at 11:15 P.M. on Friday headed for Orixíminá, a town on the Trombeta River. It had been two years since Richard had visited this church. Each time that the team held a service at the Orixíminá church, at least someone made a profession of faith. In all, 221 made professions of faith during the trip. The medical team saw a total of 1,257 patients and filled 2,576 prescriptions.

Winston and Odemeia, who would soon be moving to Manaus where he would begin his "Fish and Faith" ministry, were along on the trip as well as Little Richard and Patricia.

Since Boyd's passport and visa were late in arriving, both he and Richard had their bags packed as they met the express truck at the post office. Boyd's documents had arrived, so it was he who led a team from Harmony Heights Baptist Church of Joplin, Missouri, on a mission to the Arapiuns River Basin from July 17 to 27.

Until he arrived in Santa Rosa, Boyd was unaware of the threatened violence to lay worker Raimundinho and his wife, Euridite. Raimundinho had begun his work with AMOR as an itinerant evangelist in 1990 on the Tapajós River. In October, 1992, AMOR traveled to the Arapiuns River for its River Bank Bible Institute. The power and opposition of Satan was plainly visible, and all felt the challenge of the Arapiuns, especially Raimundinho and Euridite.

Neither Raimundinho (Little Raymond) nor Euridite had been a believer when they married at an early age. Raimundinho was the first to accept Christ, and he led his wife and son to the Lord. When Richard Walker met him in 1987, he found him a fireball for Jesus and full of love for his unbelieving brothers in Brazil. After he began his ministry with AMOR as an itinerant evangelist, Amor purchased him a small boat and he lived on the boat with his family. AMOR offered to build him a home in the village of his choice, but he chose to remain on the his boat, 9 feet by 35 feet with an 11 HP engine and no reverse gear.

It was not until May 1993, that Raimundinho pointed his *Jesus me Ama*, his new boat of 12 feet by 48 feet with a 24-horsepower motor, toward the Arapiuns. On his way, as he neared Santarém, he saw in the clouds what he perceived to be a large church building with a tiny door. As he watched, the door of the church began to enlarge and finally encompass the entire church building. He felt that this was God telling him that the door for preaching the Gospel was opening wide for him.

After stopping in Santarém, they went up the Arapiuns to the home of Euridite's parents just above the village of Santa Rosa. Here and in other villages of the Arapiuns the people were very poor, with no electricity, no stores, and very few supplies of any kind. The people also were very superstitious.

Raimundinho preached before a sizable crowd in the home of Euridite's parents and had several decisions for Christ. He felt that Santa Rosa was the place to establish a church, so he found a man there who agreed to let him preach in his home. Again a sizable crowd gathered, the service went well, and there were five more decisions. After making arrangements for a service the next night, he returned to the home of his wife's parents.

The next day a letter was delivered to him from the president and other leaders of the community. It simply stated that the village was Catholic and wanted nothing to do with Protestants. It stated that he was not welcome to come again or to preach in their village. At the appointed time for preaching in Santa Rosa the next night, Raimundinho and his family arrived, but the man who had agreed to services was out.

After asking, however, Raimundinho received permission to preach at the home of a neighbor who also had a small generator. The service began, but as the singing and preaching progressed, the president and other leaders led a large group in surrounding the house and began to yell, curse, and throw rocks at the worshipers. Despite the opposition, the service continued and several more made public their faith in Christ.

Raimundinho left that night and crossed the river to a place called Monte Sião. A small group of believers lived here but had been very timid about sharing their faith with others. They warned Raimundinho that the people did not want to hear the Gospel.

While Raimundinho was in the village, the president of Santa Rosa sent another letter by the hand of his father. This time the message was much stronger. It stated again that he was not welcome, they did not want to hear the Gospel preached, and that if he came back, this time they would kill him.

The people of Monte Sião were so scared that they begged him not to go back. But even as Apostle Paul did not heed pleas for him not to go to Jerusalem, Raimundinho told the fainthearted Christians that he would die only when God called him, and if it were to be now, that was fine with him. He said he was commissioned by God to preach the Gospel in Santa Rosa and he would be faithful to the responsibility.

At the appointed time, he started back across the river toward Santa Rosa. As he crossed, a believer traveling along with him called his attention to a strange sight in the sky. The clouds formed the shape of a very large black mountain. At the foot of the mountain was a ferocious beast that Raimundinho called a jaguar, with several heads.

To the right of the black mountain and the beast was a brilliant white cloud in the form of a horse and rider with a sword in his hand. As the white cloud approached the black cloud, the beast of the black cloud began to dissolve until the beast was no longer distinguishable. The black cloud moved away from the path of the white cloud.

The worship service that night drew a very large crowd as most of the village came out. The service progressed without any disturbance. Several more made professions of faith to bring the total to twenty-four who stood up for Christ. Twelve were baptized into the fellowship of that New Testament church.

From this group of new Christians, José Souza was chosen to be the leader of the church, while his wife, Ester, and Maria Raimundinho Santos Matos were selected to teach the children. Plans were then made for the arrival of the AMOR team on July 16.

Despite all the opposition and distractions, Raimundinho had everything ready for the mission project when the group arrived. The construction team first built a dock at Santa Rosa before going on to repaint a church at Mount Zion and reroofing a house in another village. Boyd learned that Santa Rosa had resisted the Gospel and how some of the community leaders had even threatened Raimundinho's life, but that he had continued to preach.

After the group arrived at Santa Rosa on Sunday morning, it set up its multi-ministry of medical help as well as a Bible school for the children and house-to-house evangelism. Also, a small team helped an old man reroof his house.

During the week as the team worked, treating the people and just loving them in the name of Jesus, the leaders of the village came to Raimundinho one by one and each asked forgiveness for the way they had treated him. They wanted to know how they could help him. They even offered the Catholic church as a meeting place. They confessed that they had never seen anything like what was taking place. They were being loved and helped and taught the Gospel by the very ones whom they had resisted and persecuted.

They declared, "We have never seen anything like this before!"

After moving on to Curí on Thursday, the team found an elderly couple who were the only professing Christians in town. Nicolas, eighty-three, was recovering from malaria, so the group decided to reroof his house.

When the team left Santa Rosa, a small number of people was still waiting to see the dentist. When told that there would be less than half a dozen, Boyd agreed to see them Friday night during service in Curí. While he and a dentist pulled teeth, two preached at the services. By midnight, 67 teeth had been extracted and 10 professions of faith made.

In addition to starting a new work, the group baptized 18, had 118 decisions, treated 1,097 medical patients, extracted 747 teeth, gave out 505 pairs of eyeglasses, and had an average of 250 in Vacation Bible School.

Boyd traveled on ahead, but while the remainder of the Joplin group was preparing to leave Santarém for the States, they met Richard arriving in Santarém for the Baixo Amazonas Associational meeting in Aveiro. As they hugged Richard, they expressed how much they had missed him but said that it was their best trip of the three in a row. Richard had an opportunity to visit with Winston, Odemeia, and his two grandchildren, but he missed the company of Bea, who could not travel with him. The boat was loaded with pastors when he left for Aveiro.

"Beautiful. Again, I say—BEAUTIFUL!" Richard wrote after getting his first look at the new clinic and doctor's office in Aveiro on Friday, July 29. With no hotels or motels, people were camped out or being put up in homes as the excitement grew for the Associational meeting and the dedication of the "clinic."

The sign for the clinic arrived by boat Friday night. As a second coat of paint was applied to the clinic on Saturday, the associational meeting moved to the yard of the clinic since it was several degrees cooler there.

Richard stopped the meeting at 3:30 P.M. As he and João Batista installed the sign "Clinica Linda AMOR" on the building. The crowd sang "Minha Patria Para Cristo" (My Country for Christ). Richard noted that the entire town had a different atmosphere. Richard had insisted upon a clean street in front of the clinic, so the entire town had cleaned its streets and had begun to take pride in their homes. As Richard prepared to leave, he felt a deep regret that Bea could not be present for the events.

Evidence of how well known AMOR's ministry to the Amazon Basin had become was shown when the last mission group of 1993 under the leadership of Boyd breezed through customs at Belém without a bag being opened. Skeet, Boyd's cousin, and Varig Airlines had covered all bases for the team from Southwood Baptist Church of Tulsa, Oklahoma, and Liberty Church of Broken Arrow, Oklahoma, to Flexal in the state of Pará for the August 6 to 17 trip.

After leaving Santarém at 11:30 A.M. on Sunday, August 7, Boyd had to pull into Mamaurú at 7:00 P.M. when the Amazon became too treacherous to navigate. The next morning he had difficulty in making the sharp curves in the journey through the creek and lost the aft flag to a tree limb, then another limb did some minor damage to the aft canvas. At "idle speed," he continued on to Flexal, a town of three thousand.

After getting off to a slow start, the team got under way and performed well. A large crowd turned out for the night service, with more hanging in from the outside than those inside, but the children remained quiet.

Boyd began his diary for Tuesday, August 10, with, "What a great morning. Everyone slept in till 6:00 A.M." The group received a burst of energy after a "Laying on of Hands" before starting the day's work. Thirty-four professions were made in the service that night.

Clínica Linda AMOR was dedicated July 31, 1993, in Aveiro on the Tapajós River in the state of Para, Brazil. Before the clinic was opened, a large region in this area of the Amazon Basin was without medical services. The hospital was paid for by the Don Carter family of Dallas, Texas, and Dr. David Shuler of Joplin, Missouri. The total cost of operation is provided by the Carter family.

These two men inspect equipment for the clinic at Aveiro in February 1994. Seated is Eugene Owen, who has also checked medical equipment for AMOR at Belterra and Fordlândia. With him is Ken McElveen, an electrician. Both are from Prairie Grove, Texas. Herb Gray, an electrician from Mountain Home, Arkansas, also worked as one of the three-man team.

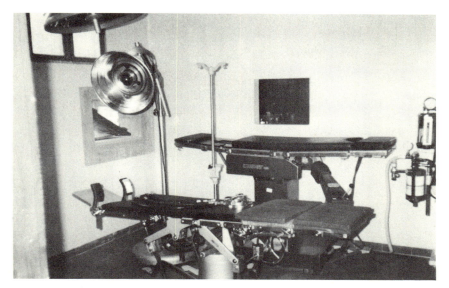
The operating room.

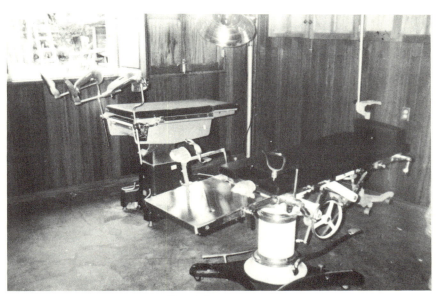
The delivery room.

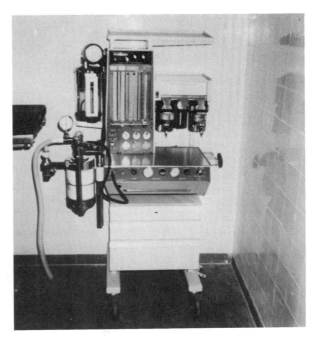

The anesthesia machine.

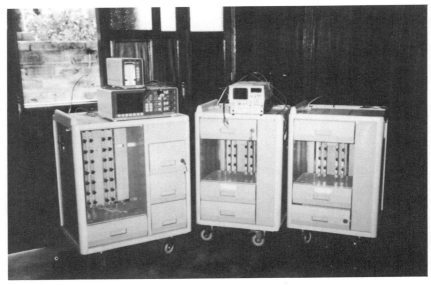

Portable heart monitors.

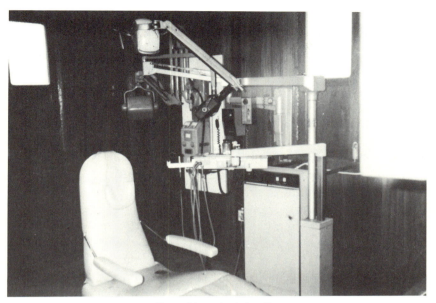

One of two dental units.

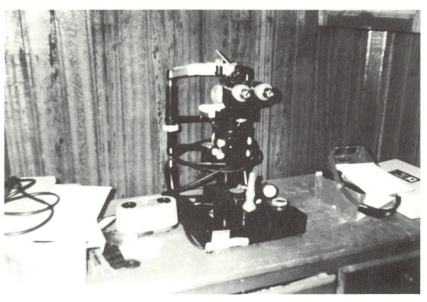

The slit lamp for optometry.

The construction team got the floor joist down during the next day. The basic foundation could not be laid in advance by John the Baptist because no funds had been received in time to purchase materials. After having to be in many other places and then acting as the only dentist, Boyd was determined to have a dentist on subsequent trips. His spirits were heightened, however, when more than 400 attended the service that night and 10 professed faith in Christ.

The team decided to leave Flexal early because several hundred people would be arriving on Friday for the annual "Acari (Bodo) Festival." Boyd felt that their services would be ineffective if they stayed. At the final service on Thursday night, 30 professed faith in Christ. A total of 23 were baptized in a brief service at 1:00 P.M. the next day at the water's edge. The group then departed for Matá.

Boyd recorded God's intervention in this manner:

> We left the main creek channel at a cut-off that was to lead us to Matá. As we passed in front of a small village, our guide lost the narrow channel. We ran aground. I pulled off, regrouped and tried again in a new direction. We ran aground again.
>
> Once more we pulled off. By this time, I was becoming a bit enraged! We were running out of daylight and I really wanted to reach our destination. Each time we ran aground, the village to our right became ever more looming in the distance. We attempted one more time to find the channel, but to no avail. It became at that very moment crystal clear to me that we were to drop anchor right here at this village.
>
> Rick, Skeet, Kurt and I boarded the *Apóstolo Mateus* and headed for shore. What a beautiful, receptive people! The most amazing thing is that the name of this village is Matá! The village we thought was Matá is named Silencio.
>
> We arranged for the school and dance hall for tomorrow's work day and they asked us to have a service tonight! I think that the most beautiful manifestation of God's design was that when we took the *Beatriz* in closer to shore for the service, we passed through the same area where we kept running aground, but this time with 18 feet of water!

Boyd, indeed, felt confirmation that God had intervened, as a leader of the community was among those making professions of faith.

Boyd's hands were bruised from the accumulated days of handling the dental instruments. Others in the group showed the effects of working hard all week.

The team worked until noon Sunday before leaving Matá for a two-hour trip to Mamaurú where services were held that night. After services they headed down the mighty Amazon for the trip to Santarém. Total visible results of the trip showed 160 decisions for Christ, a 433 average in Vacation Bible School, 23 baptisms, 412 teeth extracted, 1,213 patients seen, 207 pairs of eyeglasses fitted, and a temple constructed.

Much work still remained as preparations were made for 1994, but the River Bank Bible Institute from November 23 to December 7 would complete AMOR's main activities in the Lower Amazon Valley for 1993. With 55 students from 23 different churches aboard and sleeping in the same space in which fewer volunteers from the States had felt cramped, Richard declared this to be the best institute yet.

He stated the threefold purpose of the institute was (1) to train lay pastors in the knowledge and practice of God's Word; (2) to promote fellowship, Christian love, and understanding among the churches and pastors; (3) to seek together, as God's called-out servants, the powerful, searching, cleansing, reviving, transforming work of God's Holy Spirit upon God's people and this wicked world.

He wrote: "Beyond a doubt, these three purposes are being worked out by our precious Lord in The Lower Amazon Valley of Brazil. We see more evidence each Institute of God's hand in answering our prayers."

In 1993, the 23 Brazilian churches represented started the year with 425 members, with an average of 1,150 in attendance each time they met together to worship. They baptized 238 during the year and finished the year with 663 members. Richard concluded: "That is a ratio of one baptism for each 1.7 members. At this ratio, the Southern Baptist Convention would baptize 7,865,165 this year. You figure it out for your church."

The pastors planned even greater things in 1994 as they set goals to baptize 498 and to have 1,875 average in attendance. The most exciting thing was that they committed themselves to start 42 new works in 1994.

Richard summed up his feelings:

> The Institute was an immeasurable inspiration to us. We feel at this point that God is directing Bea and me to give more time to this ministry. Boyd is able to pick up more of the load of directing the missionary trips from the States. We seek God's guidance in planning and financing the River Bank Bible Institute. We need to have *three* different groups of pastors studying *twice* each year. A lot of time and a great deal of financing, *BUT GOD IS ABLE* (Eph. 3:20–21).

When they were not engaged in their various assignments ashore, the volunteers to Brasilia Legal from the First and Second Baptist churches of Arkadelphia spent their time on board a rented launch.

Dr. Richard Walker preaches at a night service in the still-to-be-completed mahogany wood sanctuary at Brasilia Legal.

Eluardo, Brazilian pastor (far left), and Richard Walker (far right) baptize believers in the blue waters of the Tapajós River at the conclusion of the mission to Brasilia Legal.

Citizens of Brasilia Legal erect a sign ("Brasilia Legal thanks you") to show their appreciation to the American volunteers. Many came aboard the launch to bid emotional farewells.

Chapter 21

Early in 1994 AMOR finally had its long-awaited, fully operational hospital after three Arkansans journeyed to Aveiro on February 1 to 15 to install equipment. Two men from Prairie Grove were Eugene Owen, a medical technician who had also checked equipment for AMOR at Belterra and Fordlândia, and Ken McElveen, an electrician. Herb Gay, an electrician from Mountain Home, also worked with the team.

The trio installed equipment for the examining room, the operating room, the delivery room, and an anesthesia machine. They set up a portable heart monitor, a laboratory, and a pharmacy. In addition, they installed two dental units and a slit lamp for optometry.

Opposition from Foreign Mission Board–appointed missionaries in Brazil still occasionally reared its head. Since some specific rather than the usual vague charges had been brought against him, Richard decided to face them head on. When he arrived in Santarém to begin his first trip of the year from April 12 to 23, he first requested a meeting with the Brazilian pastors and the persons making the charges. After Richard answered each charge, the Brazilian Association and pastors decided the persons bringing the charges needed an attitude change and the Association planned action to bring about the change.

With the air cleared as far as the Association was concerned, Richard was glad to leave Santarém and begin the work he felt God had sent him to do in Óbidos with the group from Twin Lakes Baptist Church from Mountain Home, Arkansas.

The Brazilian doctors welcomed the group warmly and the surgeon there gave them complete control of the operating room. The mayor donated the use of a bus to transport them and supplies around town. Bible school was a riot, with more than a thousand students, so the teachers divided them into a morning and an afternoon group.

At the second worship service, there was no response to the invitation. Richard prayed and rebuked Satan, then offered the invitation again. This time, twenty came forward and confessed Christ as Savior.

Saturday's attendance of 1,850 in Bible school caused chaos, so Richard announced that no presents, including caps, would be given at the conclusion. On Sunday, attendance dropped to 850.

Richard saw many sad cases as he made house calls. One family that had seven grown, normal children also had three sons who were pituitary dwarfs. One age 31 and another age 30 were under thirty inches in height and had the mental capacity of less than a one-year-old. Naked, they sat on the floor. Their heads were adorned with beautiful black hair. A fourteen-year-old was the size of a 5-to-7-year-old and had much less mental capacity. He could walk but not talk.

At another house, Richard found a twenty-seven-year-old woman whose skin was scaly and flaky all over. She had been that way since birth. He hoped that the Kenelog they left with her would help.

The medical team saw 1,410 patients and performed 50 surgeries. A total of 13 of these were general; 10 were cataracts and 27 pterygiums were removed. A total of 2,526 prescriptions were filled and 1,328 teeth extracted, while pairs of eyeglasses fitted totaled 540. Ninety-eight made decisions for Christ.

Before beginning the sixth annual River Bank Bible Institute, Richard and Boyd checked on *Clinica Linda AMOR* in Aveiro and found everything going well. While there, they received a request from the workers of the area to take their next team to Cuparí, one of the poorest places AMOR had worked in.

Despite their substandard existence, the workers there had cut logs to begin building their church. AMOR committed to buying lumber to finish the church, and Boyd would lead a team there from May 31 to June 11.

As Richard prepared to leave Santarém for the Institute, he received an uplifting sendoff, which provided a glorious tone to the beginning. Ribamar, the man who made jewelry and brought it to the *AMOR Beatriz* to sell to the groups, talked at length with Boyd and Richard about the need that he and his wife felt in their hearts and home for Jesus.

After Richard returned from taking Boyd to the airport, Ribamar and his wife, Cely, picked him up at the boat at 8:00 P.M. and took him to their home. There he talked with the couple, along with their thirteen-year-old daughter, Ribamar's brother and his live-in girl friend, and a twelve-year-old nephew, as well as a five-year-old daughter. As they bowed in prayer two hours later, all of the adults stood and confessed aloud repentance and faith in Christ.

Thirty-eight happy and excited lay workers boarded the *Beatriz* at Santarém, while two stayed behind to bring three workers coming from an Indian tribe in an isolated, distant place called Jacarécanga. In addition to these five, 13 more from up river on the Arapiuns brought the total lay workers to a record 56; and the crew members made a grand total of 69 aboard. Nobody complained, however, about the crowded boat.

Also aboard from Manaus was sixty-seven-year-old Pastor Darciso, executive secretary for the Amazonas Baptist Convention. The convention had asked Richard to assist it in the area of River Bank Bible Institute, but the people who had told it about AMOR's work had not been very complimentary.

After observing firsthand, Pastor Darciso was 100 percent convinced that what AMOR was doing was right and of the Lord. He stated publicly that what he had seen was what he had dreamed would be a reality in his state. He said when he returned home, he would strongly state the truth of AMOR's work in Pará.

Richard commented:

> It is amazing to me how people all over Brazil seem to be compelled to have an opinion about our work. Ninety-nine percent of them have never seen first-hand, nor even talked to anyone who has actually participated with us. But a strong opinion they have, and enjoy sharing it with others!
>
> The opinions are nearly always derogatory and totally wrong. For instance, the pastor who is with us from Jacarécanga a long ways from here or anywhere else, up the Tapajós River among the Indians. He wanted his laymen to receive some training to help them assume the

work there. He is sick and there is no "trained" pastor who will live where he has led for 30 years.

Just before the trip here, some pastor went by to see him. I don't want to know who it was. He discouraged this pastor with information that was totally false. He is now a 100 percent convert and will send some of the men from his church each time we have RBBI. Praise God, this work continues to grow!

Boyd led a group from Russellville, Arkansas, and Orlando, Florida, to Cuparí, Santa Cruz, and Apací from May 31 to June 11. The villagers at Cuparí relieved his worries since they had already built shelves in the pastor's home for the pharmacy and had constructed steps up the steep, slippery bank.

The people here were some of the poorest that Boyd had ever seen. The pastor's home, which the medical team would use, was a small, dark mud hut, while the eye clinic was a hundred yards away in the "school house," a pole building with a thatched roof. Since the dental team had no place to work, it decided to work on the *Beatriz*.

Raimundinho showed up unexpectedly from Santarém on the third day at Cuparí and took the evangelism team down river for the day. They returned at 4:45 P.M. and announced two decisions for Christ. The construction team decided to finish the outside of the building and let the local people put up the paneling.

Most of the group stayed up late Saturday after a wonderful worship service and a surprise birthday for a young woman of the team on her sixteenth birthday. The construction team was up late sawing and hammering on the roof of the building.

After working on the building and seeing everyone who came for medical treatment Sunday, the team baptized seven at a 3:00 P.M. service and dedicated the temple that night. Then the construction team worked late into the night and almost completed the building. Now, Boyd felt that it was time to move on to Santa Cruz to meet a request from there.

Despite having been up late that night, the group was up by 5:00 A.M. and was under way for Aveiro by 6:00 A.M. Dr. Waldemar and his wife were there to meet them. Boyd and he discussed many things, and Boyd rejoiced that he and his wife would vacate permanently on Wednesday.

Boyd wrote: "All of our problems are resolved—PTL! It just took a face-to-face encounter in order for them to understand the realities of authority, mission, purpose, and accountability that they had refused to recognize up to this point."

Boyd closed the hospital and placed Pastor Pedro and his wife in charge of maintenance until AMOR had restructured the operation. She was a lab technician and would receive instructions from Dr. Waldemar on how to keep the equipment clean and operational during what was thought would be a brief closure.

Arriving at Santa Cruz at eleven that morning, the team ate lunch and went to work immediately. The ophthalmologist did four pterygiums, while the medical work included the removal of a fingernail and the evangelism team traveled many miles. A total of 206 turned out for Bible school. A night service was held in the park, with Boyd translating for Raimundinho. Boyd said it was the best sermon he had ever preached!

After working hard the next morning, the team left for Apací where Rainmundinho had received a request. Arriving at 3:30 P.M., the team found that the village had apparently been built on the universe's fire ant factory. Nevertheless, the volunteers set up and worked until 6:00 P.M. Boyd perceived a warmth here and felt the group really needed more than the time allotted.

Nevertheless, after working through the next day, the group pulled up anchor at 1:30 A.M. Thursday and arrived in Santarém at 9:30 A.M. The ophthalmologist performed one more duty as he did a cataract lens implant on the eye of Raimundinho. He had been injured in that eye when he was twelve years of age and almost immediately he could not see out of it. The ophthalmologist said a cataract had grown over it.

In addition to 23 decisions and 7 baptisms during the multiple-mission trip, the medical team had seen 1,020 patients and removed 12 pterygiums, while the dental team had extracted 802 teeth. Construction finished the church building at Cuparí.

When the AMOR team from the First Baptist Church of Murray, Kentucky, arrived in Manaus for a June 14–26 trip, Richard noticed that the customs official was having every passenger's bag opened. He held the team back until the end, then the twenty-nine persons approached the officials with their bags.

The official pointed to one bag and wanted to know what was in it. Richard summoned the owner, Dan Shipley, who said it contained soap and tweezers. When the official received the same answer for the second bag, he asked whether they were all doctors. Richard explained the makeup of the group, so the official waved them through without opening a bag.

The team had busy work days at Lago Campo Alegre on the Cuminá River. In addition to holding Bible school and having worship services, they saw many medical, dental, and optometry patients. One woman had been scalped by the propeller of a boat. Richard realized she was lucky to be alive and promised to bring her a wig when he returned in July. The Secretary of Health from Oriximiná visited and was so impressed that he decided to stay all week.

The dentist told this on himself. He had deadened one side of a boy's face, then moved on to anesthetize other patients. When he returned to the boy, he proceeded to remove root pieces from the side he had not deadened. The dentist said the boy did not flinch, but he doubted that the lad would return for another treatment!

The medical team saw 1,236 patients, the dentist extracted 681 teeth, and 460 pairs of eyeglasses were fitted. A total of 15 made decisions and 21 were baptized.

A local battle over where the medical clinic would be set up appeared imminent when the team from the First Baptist Church of Paducah, Kentucky, arrived in Oriximiná for its July 5–13 trip. The wife of the mayor was head of the Department of Social Work there and wanted it set up in her building, while the town doctor had already set it up in his clinic. The doctor, apparently not wanting to fight with the mayor's wife, solved the problem by taking off for his farm.

With that problem resolved, the optometrist, dentist, and the two "family practice" physicians (a cardiologist and an obstetrician-gynecologist) began to take care of what appeared to be thousands of patients. Crowd control, as usual in such situations, was a problem because the people were afraid they would not be seen by the doctors.

Several people were at the boat before the medical team went to the clinic the next morning. Among them was the woman from the last trip in Cuminá who had been scalped. Dr. Jerry Edwards of Murray, Kentucky, had sent her a wig and she was thrilled to get it. She was beaming in the pictures the group took of her. The young ophthalmologist did an excellent job on a cataract lens implant even though the difficult operation was performed under less than ideal circumstances.

Dr. Lloyd Housman, the obstetrician-gynecologist, discovered two women, one with an advanced case of cancer of the cervix and another with an advanced case of ovarian cancer. Both families were told that their loved one had only three months to live.

As the service in the park concluded Friday night and as the invitation was being given, Richard looked at the crowd as he prayed. He saw that several raised their hands to indicate acceptance of Christ as their Savior. Some young people punched each other and began to laugh. Richard stopped the service and told them that when they made fun like this, they were doing it to God and would have to answer to Him. He told them that they had better be careful because God would chastise them for it. He continued the invitation and eleven young people came forward to accept Christ.

The team decided to back away from the power struggle between the mayor's wife and the Secretary of Health as to who would get in to see the doctor. Despite this, things went well and the team was able to help many physically. The mayor and his wife had not attended any of the services, but the mayor hosted a dinner for the team Saturday evening in a restaurant owned by one of the church members.

The local woman who kept the door at the optometry/dental clinic ordered the people around and humiliated them. Pastor Kevin McCallon tried to witness to her, but she told him she did not believe in God. At the end of the week, however, she handed him a note she had written. It said, "After seeing such marvelously, loving people as you, I have believed now in God and have given my life to Jesus and I am convinced that we will meet again someday."

Richard closed his journal as follows:

> It's so very hard to close the clinic to leave. A lady held up her sick baby to Winston, begging him to have a doctor look at her. People pulling, pushing and begging to "just see one more." It's easy to forget

the spiritual part of a mission like this. It's been very difficult, but good week.

This week the doctors treated 1,347 patients, there were 10 eye surgeries, 297 teeth extracted, 125 eyeglasses fitted. There were 20 public decisions made for the Lord and an average daily Bible School attendance of 185.

"To God be the glory, great things HE has done!"

Boyd led the group from Harmony Heights Baptist Church of Joplin, Missouri, on the July 19–30 trip to Santa Rosa on the Arapiuns River. This was the third consecutive year for this church and some of the group had made five to six trips in all. This church had accepted the challenge of the Arapiuns River basin to evangelize there and nurture the Gospel. They supported Pastor Raimundinho and maintained his boat. They even took care of the emergencies that occurred during the year.

When the team reached Santa Rosa at 8:30 on the morning of Thursday, July 21, Boyd found that Satan had been very busy in the village. Apparently the leaders of the village had forgotten how they had apologized to Raimundinho after seeing the loving ministry of a previous group. The church had eighty members, but the leaders of the village were adamantly opposed to the construction of a church building. They had threatened the lady who had given the land, Raimundinho, and the builder Assisi at knife point. Boyd chose not to divulge this to the team at that time. He joked dryly, "These are the situations that tend to relax one . . ."

All teams were on location and working by 10:30 A.M. Despite not being expected until the next day, they saw a large number of patients and had a good worship service that night.

Raimundinho related an incredible story to Boyd. After he and the others had been threatened a number of days before, the church members decided to pray. They prayed every morning at five and every evening for three days that the Holy Spirit would bind Satan from this place. After these days of praying, a man mysteriously came from the jungle wearing a very large machete. No one had ever seen him before. He went directly to the building site and demanded to speak to the person in charge. Raimundinho confronted him and asked him what he needed. The man replied, "When Satan is loosed in this place, all of this will be finished once and for all." The man then walked into the jungle and has not been seen since. Raimundinho and Boyd were both convinced that this person was a messenger of Satan, one who confessed that Satan was indeed bound in this place as an answer to prayer and supplication.

While most of the team labored at Santa Rosa, some of the team took the smaller boat, *Jesus Me Ama*, to Curí. The clinic did not close until 11:00 P.M. on Saturday. Seventeen made decisions for Christ at the worship service that night. The *Beatriz* anchored under what Boyd described as "the most beautiful full moon in the universe."

With the local people restless because they knew it was the team's last day, the volunteers worked through lunch period on Sunday, then had no time to shower and eat before worship service. Nineteen were baptized and the church building dedicated. The building looked impressive even though the construction team ran out of siding. Assisi, one of the participants, would complete the work.

The team found an entirely different spirit, a sweet one, at Maró, a community almost at the foot of the falls. Boyd took his "first and last" jungle walk that morning. He apparently was not impressed: "Gee, what a thrill. Let me see, we saw round trees, square trees, short trees, tall trees, skinny trees . . ."

Pastor Tim Sumners wrote in his log book: "This trip provided several 'firsts' for us. It was the first time to share communion with Brazilian people; first time to see a newly constituted church; first time to return to the same area; first time to play soccer with the village people; and the first time we enjoyed the Brazilians' innovation in air travel, i.e., the best way home is to go 2,000 miles south from here before going north! Now why couldn't USA airlines think of this!!!"

A total of 120 made decisions during the trip, 19 were baptized, an average of 125 attended Bible school, 904 patients were seen, 2146 prescriptions were filled, 1304 teeth were extracted, 186 pairs eyeglasses were fitted, a temple was built in Santa Rosa and the Catholic Church was painted in Maró.

After a twenty-seven-month absence because of illnesses, Bea was finally able to return to Brazil with her husband on a mission trip to Terra Santa in the state of Pará from August 2 to 11. Dr. Al

Harvey had been on four previous trips with AMOR, but this would be his first in the leadership role as he directed the group from Oklahoma City.

For Bea, it was her first time to get a brief visit with Winston and his family, Odemeia, and the two grandchildren, Richard II and Patricia. She was glad they had moved back to Santarém. Winston would accompany them on the trip. She thought the *Beatriz* was crowded when it left Santarém with 55 aboard, but en route the group picked up a pastor in Óbidos; Dr. Dantas, a dentist who was Secretary of Health; and the mayor of Terra Santa, a town of 13,000 just off the Nhamundá River.

After a nineteen-hour boat ride, the volunteers agreed upon work sites and were soon at work. No construction team came with this group. Dr. Edward Glinski, ophthalmologist, would have an air-conditioned room in which to do cataract lens implants and pterygiums. He had brought along an auto refractor and had trained his daughter to use it. After assessing the eyeball, the machine spat out the prescription for the eyeglasses.

The dental team was swamped, with as many as 290 teeth extracted in one day. The medical team kept busy with minor surgeries. Cataract lens implants and pterygium removals were done each day.

Just how medically destitute the three-county area of 45,000 people with no doctor was, was illustrated by a man who met Richard and Bea as they went into the clinic. Bea related his story:

> He lives in a very isolated village and he's going blind. Last April, he heard there was a group of Americans in Óbidos, and doctors were there. He set out walking, but when he arrived, the team had already left. He was told that another group of Americans would be in Campo Alegre in June.
>
> He determined to go there. He thought he was giving himself plenty of time for the walk, but when he got there, the team had just left. He learned that still another group would be in Oriximiná in July, so again went, and again he missed them. The pastor there told him a group would be in Terra Santa in August.
>
> Today he arrived, and the Americans are still here! Tomorrow he will have surgery! We praise God for bringing together the need and the answer to the need.

He had pterygiums removed from each eye and the operations were successful.

The mayor of Terra Santa requested AMOR to send another team the next year "exactly like this one."

Of the interaction between the team members and the Brazilians, Bea wrote:

> A beautiful young lady holding a baby boy in her arms, a dentist and his assistant walking towards the boat with a young girl walking between them holding their hands, a hundred children chanting the names of the different team members, the near fights occurring between the children as they all try to encircle and touch an American, and on and on, it goes. This team has certainly "reached out and touched" during these days.

Services were held in the park each night. In all, 21 made decisions for Christ. Bible School had an average attendance of 491, with 980 attending the final session. The Eye Clinic fitted 559 pairs of glasses, did 9 cataract lens implants, and performed 27 pterygiums.

The dentists extracted 1,655 teeth, while the medical team saw 819 patients and filled 1,638 prescriptions. In addition to the Brazilian dentist, Dr. Carlos Consulmagno, an ophthalmologist making his fourth trip with AMOR, came all the way from São Paulo.

Chapter 22

What was planned as the "Grand Finale" of seven years of taking volunteer mission groups threatened for some time to be anything else but. After several months of what Boyd Walker termed "devastating" clashes of personalities and attitudes among some of the team members, contentions seemed to be healed by the time 22 volunteers from Prestonwood Baptist Church of Dallas departed for an August 23–September 1 trip to Jurutí and Mamarú.

It would be Prestonwood's fourth consecutive AMOR trip, and Boyd was looking forward to working on a trip with his dad for the first time in three years. Boyd considered the group dynamic in its makeup of excellent medical personnel and an aggressive evangelism team.

After stopping in Óbidos to pick up Pastor Dorinilson to assist in evangelism, it was a twelve-hour ride for the group up the Amazon from Santarém to Jurutí, a heavily populated area that up to now had been indifferent to evangelistic efforts. Boyd and Richard were surprised by the excellent facilities and equipment of the air-conditioned hospital that had no one to make it work.

The group ate lunch on board the boat the first day, but after that arranged for sack lunches to be sent to the hospital as the crowds were so large. They slept in port because the river was 100 feet deep and the anchor rope was only 103 feet long.

The lines at the hospital seemed immeasurable and one doctor performed seven surgeries in one day. The eye clinic benefitted from the purchase of the auto refractor brought on the previous trip and the purchase by the present group of a lensometer that would read the prescriptions on glasses.

Services were held in the park each night, with a total of 219 making public professions of faith in Christ. Bible school showed a steady increase in attendance, with 200 by the second day and finally averaging out to 547.

At the request of a layman from Igarapé Açu, a physician and assistants, a few Bible school teachers, and Boyd and his company as a dental team went by truck to the little village about fifty miles away. The medics saw more than 200 patients, Boyd pulled 64 teeth, and 200 attended Bible school. As they rode back, the group had to duck low in the truck to keep from being hit by flying bugs.

Boyd was impressed by the work of the surgeon and staff, especially in ministering to a man who had been stabbed in the chest and was nearly bleeding to death internally. The team drained three quarts of the man's own blood from his chest, then put it back into him by means of an IV.

In all, the medical team saw 1,298 patients, with 28 surgeries and filled 2,596 prescriptions. A total of 497 teeth were extracted and 525 pairs of eyeglasses fitted.

While this was the last group of volunteers for 1994, Richard would conduct two River Bank Bible Institutes before the end of the year.

After having to go through the legal proceedings of releasing the crew of the *Beatriz* because it was too expensive to keep them during the inactive months, Richard was emotionally and physically drained when he arrived in Óbidos with 22 students and five teachers for the seventh River Bank Bible Institute from September 13 to 28. He did get to visit in Santarém with Winston, Odemeia, Richard II, and Patricia.

Richard had invited the Santarém pastors and their wives to have lunch aboard the *Beatriz*. Only one pastor was absent, but local missionaries turned down their special, personal invitations. Richard was surprised when one Brazilian pastor who had viciously opposed their work only four years ago told how he had received his first impression of Richard and his call to the ministry at an institute held in the 1960s. He went on for a long time about how important the work of AMOR was, especially the River Bank Bible Institute.

Many of those who had been trained in previous institutes were able to act as teachers in the seventh one. Three of the pastors preached during the night services. One of these services was lit only by a full moon, but resulted in 20 decisions. With 42 total decisions, nine baptisms in Óbidos and six in Santa Maria, the ordination of a pastor, and the constitution of a church, Richard felt that the institute had been a wonderful success.

Richard saw his latest grandson, four-week-old Rodrigo Samuel, for the first time as he visited with Winston and family in Santarém before conducting the eighth River Bank Bible Institute from November 1 to 14.

After leaving port at noon on December 2 for Aveiro, Richard had hoped to get past the big rocks in the Tapajós River before dark. When he didn't, he cut his speed and traveled very carefully since there was no moon. He decided to drop anchor and wait for the line boat so he could follow it, but it came up the other side of the river. After making radio contact, Richard was assured that the *Beatriz* was already past the rocks. He continued on and arrived in Aveiro at 4:00 A.M.

A group of 43 lay workers and 3 Brazilian pastor professors began their teaching/learning, but not Richard, who woke up quite ill at 5:00 A.M. This was the first time in thirty years of working up and down the rivers that Richard had been seriously ill, but everything seemed to hit him at once and no medicine was available. A pastor bought some medicine at a little pharmacy and wanted Richard to take it intravenously, but Richard declined.

Richard realized for the first time how so many of Brazilians in the lower Amazon region felt when they became sick. He had always said that when a Brazilian got sick in the jungle, he either got well or he died. Now he thought about the many who had spent days in pain and sickness while their wives had to provide fish and take care of the sick husband.

Richard, bitterly ill for the next two days, spent much of that time praying fervently that God would provide a living for the workers. He prayed that God would keep the porpoise out of their fishing nets and the piranhas from destroying the nets. He prayed that God would put enough fish into their nets to feed their families.

Friday was a complete blank for Richard, but he had recovered enough by Saturday so that he was able to talk business with José João, an associate pastor of a Presbyterian church in Manaus. Since this church had a clinic boat ministry, Richard wanted to discuss their helping AMOR find medical personnel and an administrator for the Clínica Linda AMOR in Aveiro.

Pastor Pedro and his wife had been taking care of the hospital during the interim period. It was in excellent condition, having been repainted, spotlessly clean, with a beautiful yard and garden. Pastor José found the equipment better than any in Manaus except the large hospital there, and was excited about the possibilities of getting a doctor, or perhaps several, to give time throughout each year.

A year previously each of the workers had set a goal for the year. Their goal for baptisms was 455 and they actually baptized 334. Total average attendance in worship was set at 1,453 and the results were 1,742 worshiping each week in 50 locations. They set a goal of opening 27 new churches and started 22 new works for the total of 50. Their goals for 1995 were 614 baptisms, 2,520 in attendance in all the churches, and to open 33 new churches.

Were the three 1994 institutes worth the investment of $34,800? Richard points out that each of the 122 students cost $285.25 per student and each received four weeks of Bible study and practical experience. For the $20,400 investment in pastoral aid, one soul was won and baptized for each $165.26.

Richard adds: "The real return is the commitment and joy that is so evident in the lives of these workers. They have so little, yet give so much. . . ."

The Walkers themselves had given seven years of their lives in ministering to the spiritual and physical needs in the remote areas of the lower Amazon valley. Our journal of the Amazon Mission Organization will end with 1994, but the story of AMOR is a continuing story that many generations of Walkers are likely to continue in one form or another in the future. Richard II is the oldest and Samuel the youngest of Winston's and Odemeia's three children; and William, Phillip, and Matthew, the three sons of Boyd and Cida, make a total of five grandsons. Patricia is Richard's and Bea's only granddaughter. As they worked together on their last 1994 trip with volunteers, Richard and Boyd were already planning the 1995 budget and how they could fine-tune the program after seven years. In fact, Richard conducted revival services at the Second Baptist Church in Manaus, site of his first mission assignment, during January 13–23, 1995.

During the past seven years, 50 trips taking 1,046 volunteers had been made with 29 new works begun. Decisions for Christ totaled 3,673, with 458 baptisms. A daily average of 435 had attended Bible School. Construction teams had built 24 churches, one home for a physician, a medical clinic, two education annexes, three parsonages, and two prayer gazebos.

Medical teams had seen 41,808 patients, performed 179 surgeries, including 24 cataract extractions with lens implants and 179 pterygiums removed, and filled 112,013 prescriptions. Optometry had fitted 10,833 eyeglasses, and dentists had extracted 25,222 teeth. Eight River Bank Institutes helped 35 interior churches while training 218 lay pastors.

In addition to the *AMOR-Beatriz*, other boats provided included the *AMOR-Patrice, Swink, Roy Ruby, Jesus Me Ama I, Mateus, J. Adams, and Jesus Me Ama II*. Although persons of other denominations had accompanied volunteers on the trips, either Baptist churches or private groups had served as sponsors. In 1994, however, the work became truly ecumenical when First United Methodist Church of Joplin, Missouri, became a sponsor.

Perhaps the work of the Richard Walkers may be summed up best by Richard's own definition of love (AMOR) he has printed on souvenir cups: "Love is the unsolicited giving of the best you have on behalf of another regardless of response."

AMOR in '95

125 volunteers	2,535 teeth extracted
5 trips	2,572 eyeglasses fitted
2 workers' institutions	75 pterygium surgeries
211 professions	14 cataract surgeries
271 avg VBS attendance	15 general surgeries
3,735 patients treated	4 constructions
6,175 prescriptions filled	

'96 AMOR Opportunities
(If interested in serving on one of the following trips, contact AMOR at 1-800-307-4884 ASAP)

March 11-22: AMOR RBBI, Urara River.
May 13-24: Orlando, Fl, FBC, Jurutí Velho, Amazon River.
May 27-June 7: Mountain Home, AR, Twin Lakes Baptist, Óbidos, Amazon River.
June 1-12: Murray, KY, FBC Lago Salgado, Cuminá River.
July 15-26: Dallas TX, Fellowship, Autazes, Parana do Mamori.
August 5-16: Prestonwood Baptist, Dallas TX, Terra Santa, Nhamunda River.
August 19-30: Joplin, MO, Cooperative Effort, Manaquiri, Amazon River.
September 9-20: AMOR RBBI, Lago Grande, Amazon River.
October 7-18: Orlando Grace, Orlando, Fl, Tapuru, Purus River.
June 10-21: Russellville, AR, FBC, Jurutí, Amazon River.

Believe in Angels?
by Richard Walker in 1995

As the group from Mountain Home started their trek to Miami, (with their final destination being Óbidos) "Hurricane Erin" was threatening Florida. The Miami airport was virtually closed, encouraging cancellation of all flights out of Memphis to Miami. By faith, the group insisted on flying anyway and soon after their arrival in Miami, the airport closed. Dentist Charlie Hartsfield and daughter Emily did not make it for the Varig flight which had left five hours earlier for Brazil. In addition, sixteen large action packer bags containing important medical supplies had not flown out with the first group and were still in Memphis. An employee of Varig Airlines, Faye McDonald, was doing everything possible to be helpful routing Charlie and Emily to Santarem through Sao Paulo. This meant getting twenty bags through customs where the officials were unfamiliar with AMOR, a feat thought to be a long-shot. However, this was thought to be easier than going through Rio. Meanwhile, the rest of the group were already in Santarem and were both concerned and deep in prayer about both the Hartsfields and the needed medical equipment.

On the plane to San Paulo, a beautiful young lady sat next to Charlie and Emily. She was very friendly, and put them both at ease as she spoke both English and Portuguese perfectly. She stayed to help them retrieve all twenty bags at the baggage claim, and helped them through customs. Amazingly not a bag was opened nor a question asked. After they had checked in for flights to Manaus and Santarem, their "friend" just faded into the crowd and was not seen again. To the relief of everyone, Charlie, Emily and the twenty bags finally arrived. The work was begun on time, and God's mission was fulfilled. The Bible speaks of God's angels watching over His children. At least to Charlie and the rest of the praying group, God had certainly sent an angel that day.

．．．． Some have entertained angels without knowing it.
—Hebrews 13:2

Epilogue

The primary purpose of this chronicle is to record the life work of a dedicated family with a burning desire to take the Gospel where people in the remote areas of the Amazon River Basin have never been told of the Bible, or have never heard the Gospel preached evangelistically.

Richard and Bea Walker, along with their sons Winston and Boyd, have realized that it is not enough to *tell* about the love of Jesus Christ, but that they must *demonstrate* that love by reaching out and meeting the pressing physical needs of these people, many of whom have never had the services of a doctor, dentist, or optometrist. The Walkers have never subordinated the evangelistic purpose of their mission, but they often have overcome opposition and superstition through their ministry to physical needs.

The Walkers, first through the Amazon/Arkansas Mission Organization (AMAR) and then through the Amazon Mission Organization (AMOR), have discovered how effective volunteers can be even though they cannot speak the native language. They have used effectively the multi-purpose missions of evangelization, Bible School, medical and dental treatment, optometry, and the construction of new temples, parsonages, or education buildings, to strengthen or establish churches in remote areas.

In addition, they have used the River Bank Bible Institute, held twice annually, to train many native pastors and laymen to lead in the churches. All of this had not been done without opposition, both in Brazil and in the United States. It has brought about alienation from some people they considered their best friends, but the Walkers have continued to persevere.

As the senior Walkers move into their 60s, they realize their sons and grandchildren must eventually carry the load. But the unflagging spirit of the senior Walkers is exemplified in a quote from a note by Bea Walker to the author: "Please pray for the April 11–19 (1995) trip up the Purvis River. How exciting to go into 'new' territory!"

While many churches have repeatedly sent groups to the Amazon, new churches continue to send volunteers for the first time. While Southern Baptist churches have formed the bulk of the volunteers, groups have crossed denominational lines and come from many states. Anyone wanting to know more about the Amazon Mission Organization may write AMOR, Box 208, Murray, KY 42071, or call 1-800-307-4884.

—Claude Sumerlin

The Present-Day Walkers

Richard and Bea.

Winston and Odemia.

Boyd and Cida.

Appendix: List of Missionary Volunteers

Bible School
(Many of these also witnessed.)

Verna Allred, Harmony Heights Baptist Church, Joplin, MO, Arapiuns, 1994.
Jeff Anderson, Southwood Baptist Church, Tulsa, OK, Flexal, 1993.
Mary Arterbury, Russellville, AR, First Baptist Church, Soure, 1988.
Mary Atwood, Oklahoma City, OK, Terra Santa, 1994.
Glenda Austin, Joplin, MO, First United Methodist, Aveiro, 1994.
Susan Austin, Joplin, MO, First United Methodist, Aveiro, 1994.
Benjamin Bailey, Mountain Home, AR, Twin Lakes Baptist, Óbidos, 1993.
Carol Baker, Harmony Heights Baptist Church, Joplin, MO, Arapiuns, 1994.
Christina Baldridge, Gracemont Baptist, Tulsa, OK, Fordlândia, 1991; First Baptist, Albuquerque, NM, Aveiro, 1992.
Jan Baldridge, First Baptist, Albuquerque, NM, Fordlândia, 1990; Gracemont Baptist, Tulsa, OK, Fordlándia, 1991 (see *Optometry*).
Chris Barr, Vian Baptist, Vian, OK, Monte Sião, 1989; Prainha, 1991, at age eighty-two.
Laura Beede, Gracemont Baptist, Tulsa, OK, Itaituba, 1988.
Christy Bell, First Baptist, Murray, KY, Cuminá, 1994.
Geraldine Bell, First Baptist, Albuquerque, NM, Aveiro, 1992.
Donnie Blackmon, First Southern Baptist, Del City, OK, Terra Santa, 1990.
Pat Blair, FBC, Murray, KY, Lago Sapacuá, 1991; Santa Maria, 1992.
Nita Barnes, Gracemont Baptist, Tulsa, OK, Itaituba, 1988; Estrada Oito, 1989; Belterra, 1990.
Kechia Bentley, Russellville, AR/Orlando, FL, Cuparí, 1994.

Nancy Blomquist, Twin Lakes Baptist, Mountain Home, AR, Óbidos, 1994.
Gail Bolton, Vian Baptist, Vian, OK, Monte Sião, 1989.
Bobby Bragg, FBC, Paducah, KY, Oriximiná, 1994.
Sue Bristow, First United Methodist, Joplin, MO, Aveiro, 1994.
Betty Brown, FBC, Murray, KY, Cuminá, 1994.
Denise Brown, Viola, AR, Maicurú, 1993.
Janice Buchanan, Prestonwood Baptist Church, Dallas, TX, Castanhanduba, 1992.
Donna Bunce, Fuquay-Varina, NC, Maicurú, 1993.
Jackie Burks, Prestonwood Baptist, Dallas, TX, Mamaurú, 1991; Castanhanduba, 1992; Flexal, 1993; Jurutí, 1994.
Barbara Bush, FBC, Orlando, FL, Jurutí Velho, 1993.
Brenda Caldwell, Vian Baptist Church, Vian, OK, Monte Sião, 1989.
Rachel Caldwell, Vian Baptist, Vian, OK, Monte Sião, 1989.
Betty Carter, Harmony Heights Baptist, Joplin, MO, Arapiuns, 1993.
Lea Castor, Calvary Baptist, Joplin, MO, São Luiz, 1991.
Karen Chiles, Southwood Baptist, Tulsa, OK, Flexal, 1993; FBC, Paducah, KY, Oriximiná, 1994.
Ann Churchill, FBC, Murray, KY, Cuminá, 1994.
Cherie Chronister, FBC, Russellville, Santa Maria, 1992.
Lyndia Cochran, FBC, Murray, KY, Cuminá, 1994.
Bill Combs, FBC, Lakeland, FL, Santa Cruz, 1990 (deceased, 1991).
Maria Combs, FBC, Lakeland, FL, Santa Cruz, 1990; Aveiro, 1992.
Jera Connally, First Southern Baptist, Del City, OK, Aveiro, 1989.
Patty Cox, Harmony Heights Baptist, Joplin, MO, Tumbira, 1992.
Vilma Crain, First and Second Baptist, Arkadelphia, AR, Brasilia Legal, 1989.
Ginnie Craft, Vian Baptist, Vian, OK, Monte Sião, 1989.
Kathy Crook, FBC, Russellville, AR, Soure, 1988.
Toby Dall, Gracemont Baptist, Tulsa, OK, Itaituba, 1988.
Jonya Davis, FBC, Russellville, AR, Soure, 1988.
Mary Davis, First Southern, Del City, OK, Terra Santa, 1990.
Sandy Davis, FBC, Russellville, AR, Macapá, Amapá, 1987; Soure, 1988; FBC, Murray, KY, Barrheiras, 1988 (twelve-year-old Ronald also went); Palm Lake Baptist Association, FL, Santa Maria, 1990; FBC, Albuquerque, NM, Fordlândia, 1990.
Rosa Delgado, Coral Springs, FL, Baptist, Aveiro, 1992.

Evelyn Denton, FBC, Russellville, AR, Jurutí, 1993.
Snookie Dixon, First and Second Baptist, Brasilia Legal, 1989.
Pam Doerge, Calvary Baptist, Joplin, MO, São Luiz, 1991.
Dora Dudgeon, Twin Lakes Baptist, Mountain Home, AR, Óbidos, 1993, 1994.
Linda Ehlinger, Vian Baptist, Vian, OK, Monte Sião, 1989.
Rob Elliott, FBC, Lakeland, FL, Santa Cruz, 1990.
Tricia Elliott, Gracemont Baptist, Tulsa, OK, Estrada Oito, 1989.
Alan Ellis, Sallisaw, OK, Maicurú, 1993.
Brenda Estes, FBC, Russellville, AR, Prainha, 1991.
Rita Fabin, First United Methodist, Joplin, MO, Aveiro, 1994.
Marsue Fields, FBC, Russellville, AR, Jurutí, 1993.
Dr. Dennis Fleniken, AR/OK/TX, Santa Maria, 1992.
Nancy M. Foreman, Coral Baptist, Coral Springs, FL, Santarém, 1990.
Elaine Fulbright, Gracemont Baptist, Tulsa, OK, Itaituba, 1988; Estrada Oito, 1989; Belterra, 1990; Fordlândia, 1991; Southwood Baptist, Tulsa, OK, Flexal, 1993; Russellville, AR/Orlando, FL, Cuparí, 1994.
Dr. Pat Garnett, Coral Baptist, Coral Springs, FL, Santarém, 1990; Aveiro, 1992.
Jim Gibson, First Southern, Del City, OK, Aveiro, 1989; FBC, Lakeland, FL, Santa Cruz, 1990.
Andrea Gibson, First Southern Baptist, Del City, OK, Terra Santa, 1990.
Lindy Grief, FBC, Paducah, Ky, Oriximiná, 1994.
Lori Gulick, FBC, Russellville, AR, Soure, 1988.
Ronda Hagar, Twin Lakes Baptist, Mountain Home, AR, Óbidos, 1993, 1994.
Timothy Hardman, Twin Lakes Baptist, Mountain Home, AR, Óbidos, 1993.
Shawn Harvey, Oklahoma City, OK, Terra Santa, 1944.
Deborah Harrell, AR/OK/TX, Santa Maria, 1992.
Mark Harris, FBC, Murray, KY, Cuminá, 1994.
Steve Hatten, FBC, Murray, KY, Lago Sapacuá, 1991.
Marty High, Gracemont Baptist, Tulsa, OK, Estrada Oito, 1989.
Gretchen Hinkle, Oklahoma City, OK, Terra Santa, 1994.
Molly Hoebeke, Prestonwood Baptist, Dallas, TX, Mamaurú, 1991; Castanhanduba, 1992.

Shelby Hoebeke, Prestonwood Baptist, Dallas, TX, Castanhanduba, 1992.
Dustin Hooten, Oklahoma City, OK, Terra Santa, 1994.
Tim Houdek, Southwood Baptist, Tulsa, OK, Flexal, 1993.
Opal Howard, FBC, Murray, KY, Barrheiras, 1988.
Nelda Humphries, Calvary Baptist, Joplin, MO, São Luiz, 1991.
Marilyn Ingle, Southwood Baptist, Tulsa, OK, Flexal, 1993.
Michelle Johnson, Gracemont Baptist, Tulsa, OK, Fordlândia, 1991.
Susan Johnson, Twin Lakes Baptist, Mountain Home, AR, Óbidos, 1994.
Angela Jones, Sallisaw, OK, Maicurú, 1993.
Helen Jones, Calvary Baptist, Joplin, MO, São Luiz, 1991; Harmony Heights Baptist, Joplin, MO, Tumbira, 1992; Arapiuns, 1993.
John Jones, Prestonwood Baptist, Dallas, TX, Mamaurú, 1991.
Sue Jones, Gracemont Baptist, Tulsa, OK, Estrada Oito, 1989; Belterra, 1990.
Anna Kaplan, Prestonwood Baptist, Dallas, TX, Castanhanduba, 1992.
Lynn Kennedy, First Southern, Del City, OK, Aveiro, May 1989; December 27, 1989–January 9, 1990.
Donna Kinser, Calvary Baptist, Joplin, MO, São Luiz, 1991; Harmony Heights Baptist, Joplin, MO, Tumbira, 1992; Arapiuns, 1993, 1994.
Kelly Krause, Palm Lake, FL, Baptist Association, Santa Maria, 1990.
Kim Krause, Palm Lake, FL, Baptist Association, Santa Maria, 1990
Meg Krause, Palm Lake, FL, Baptist Association Santa Maria, 1990.
Beth LePage, Calvary Baptist, Joplin, Mo, São Luiz, 1991.
Linda Lee, FBC, Murray, KY, Cuminá, 1994.
Mickey Meyer Lemery, Gracemont Baptist, Tulsa, OK, Itaituba, 1988; Vian Baptist, Vian, OK, Monte Sião, 1989.
Nancy Lewis, Twin Lakes Baptist, Mountain Home, AR, Óbidos, 1993, 1994.
Janet Lonon, FBC, Murray, KY, 1988; Brasilia Legal, 1992.
John Lonon, FBC, Murray, KY, 1988; Palm Lake, FL, Baptist Association, Santa Maria, 1990; FBC, Russellville, AR, Prainha, 1991; AR/OK/TX, Santa Maria, 1992; FBC, Russellville, AR, Jurutí, 1993; Russellville, AR/Orlando, FL, Cuparí, 1994.
Lydia Lonon, FBC, Russellville, AR, Jurutí, 1993.

Sara Lonon, Palm Lake, FL, Baptist Association, Santa Maria, 1990.
Kris (Laina) Lovelace, Gracemont Baptist, Tulsa, OK, Estrada Oito, 1989; Belterra, 1990.
Benedita Marques, FBC, Russellville, AR, Jurutí, 1993.
Bonnie Mayes, FBC, Albuquerque, NM, Aveiro, 1992.
Rosie McPeak, Vian Baptist, Vian, OK, Monte Sião, 1989 (see *Dental*).
Jo Merrill, Russellville, AR, Prainha, 1991.
Pat Meyer, Prestonwood Baptist, Dallas, TX, Castanhanduba, 1993.
Marilyn Michail, Harmony Heights Baptist, Joplin, MO, Arapiuns, 1993.
Anthony Miller, FBC, Russellville, AR, Jurutí, 1993.
Jackie Miller, Southwood Baptist, Tulsa, OK, Flexal, 1993.
Joy Miller, FBC, Russellville, AR, Soure, 1988.
Loretta Miller, Twin Lakes Baptist, Mountain Home, AR, Óbidos, 1993, 1994.
Mike Miller, FBC, Russellville, AR, Macapá, Amapá, 1987 (see *Construction*).
Clara Faye Mitchell, FBC, Murray, KY, Cuminá, 1994.
Linda Paulette Moore, FBC, Russellville, AR, Soure, 1988.
Phyllis Moses, Gracemont Baptist, Tulsa, OK, Belterra, 1990.
Pam Murphry, FBC, Lakeland, FL, Santa Cruz, 1990.
Jason Nazarenko, Twin Lakes Baptist, Mountain Home, AR, Óbidos, 1994.
Nancy Nelson, Prestonwood Baptist, Dallas, TX, Mamaurú, 1991; Castanhanduba, 1992; Flexal, 1993; Jurutí, 1994.
Monica Nelson, Oklahoma City, OK, Terra Santa, 1994.
Andrea O'Brien, Vian Baptist, Vian, OK, Monte Sião, 1989.
Tom Olson, Twin Lakes Baptist, Mountain Home, AR, Óbidos, 1993.
Mary Overmier, FBC, Albuquerque, NM, Aveiro, 1992.
Grace Owen, Palm Lake, FL, Baptist Association, Santa Maria, July 4–15, 1990; FBC, Albuquerque, NM, Fordlândia, July 18–28, 1990.
Jeannie Parker, Russellville, AR/Orlando, FL, Cuparí, 1994.
Mrs. Karl Parker, Gracemont Baptist, Tulsa, OK, Itaituba, 1988.
Anna Marie Penix, Gracemont Baptist, Tulsa, OK, Fordlândia, 1991.
Wayne Perego, Vian Baptist, Vian, OK, Maicurú, 1993.
Wendi Perkins, Calvary Baptist, Joplin, MO, São Luiz, 1991; Maicurú, 1993.

Barbara Perryman, Viola, AR, Santa Maria, 1992.
Beth Pharo, Prestonwood Baptist, Dallas, TX, Castanhanduba, 1992.
Brit Pilgrim, FBC, Russellville, AR, Prainha, 1991; Jurutí, 1993.
Shepherd Pittman, Russellville, AR/Orlando, FL, Cuparí, 1994.
Anna Plumlee, AR/OK/FL, Santa Maria, 1992.
Tonya Polan, FBC, Albuquerque, NM, Aveiro, 1992.
Gayle Poole, Coral Baptist, Coral Springs, FL, Santarém (Maracana), 1990.
Michele Poorbaugh, FBC, Lakeland, FL, Aveiro, 1992.
Vic Porter, Twin Lakes Baptist, Mountain Home, AR, Óbidos, 1993.
Kristi Powers, Harmony Heights Baptist, Joplin, MO, Tumbira, 1992; Arapiuns, 1993.
Glenda Pruegert, First Southern, Del City, OK, Aveiro, 1989; Terra Santa, 1990.
Michael Pruegert, First Southern, Del City, OK, Terra Santa, 1990.
Alice Pruitt, FBC, Lakeland, FL, Santa Cruz, 1990.
Tim Pruett, Oklahoma City, OK, Terra Santa, 1994.
Jennifer Pugh, FBC, Russellville, AR, Jurutí, 1993.
Dan Raines, AR/OK/FL, Santa Maria, 1992.
Brenda Register, Twin Lakes Baptist, Mountain Home, AR, Óbidos, 1994.
Linda Richards, Coral Baptist, Coral Springs, FL, Santarém (Maracana), 1990.
Wanda Rio, Prestonwood Baptist Church, Dallas, TX, Mamaurú, 1991.
Betsy Robison, Vian Baptist, Vian, OK, Monte Sião, 1989.
Samatha (Miss Sam) Rocker, FBC, Lakeland, FL, Santa Cruz, 1990.
Steve Ruzie, Calvary Baptist, Joplin, MO, São Luiz, 1991.
Ray Sackett, Oklahoma City, OK, Terra Santa, 1994.
Meagan Sackett, Oklahoma City, OK, Terra Santa, 1994.
Joshua Sanford, AR/OK/FL, Santa Maria, 1992.
Ruth Scott, FBC, Russellville, AR, Soure, 1988.
Mary Shipley, First Southern, Del City, OK, Aveiro, December 27, 1989–January 7, 1990; FBC, Murray, KY, Lago Sapacuá, 1991; Cuminá, 1994.
Ken Shores, AR/OK/FL, Santa Maria, 1992.
Nicole Shurtleff, Oklahoma City, OK, Terra Santa, 1994.
Murdena Simmons, FBC, Murray, KY, Nhamundá, 1992.

Shiela Sliger, Oklahoma City, OK, Terra Santa, 1994.
Joanna Smith, Gracemont Baptist, Tulsa, OK, Fordlândia, 1991; Liberty Church, Broken Arrow, OK, Flexal, 1993; Russellville, AR/Orlando, FL, Cuparí, 1994.
Clara Stanton, Beech Street Baptist, Texarkana, AR, Jurutí, 1988.
Sylvia Taconnet, New Orleans, LA, Brasilia Legal, 1992.
Josh Tanner, FBC, Russellville, AR, Jurutí, 1993.
Stewart Taylor, Twin Lakes Baptist, Mountain Home, AR, Óbidos, 1993.
Jeanie Tilley, Russellville, AR/Orlando, FL, Cuparí, 1994.
Flo Toth, Palm Lake, FL, Baptist Association, Santa Maria, 1990.
George Townsend, Palm Lake, FL, Baptist Association, Santa Maria, 1992.
David Travis, FBC, Murray, KY, Lago Sapacuá, 1991.
Joan Turner, First Southern, Del City, OK, Aveiro, December 27, 1989–January 7, 1990.
Julia Tyckoson, Russellville, AR/Orlando, FL, Cuparí, 1994.
Susan Underwood, Beech Street Baptist, Texarkana, AR, Jurutí, 1988.
Peggy Utley, Marshall, TX, Brasilia Legal, 1992.
Deborah Waggerman, FBC, Albuquerque, NM, Fordlândia, 1990.
Joetta Ward, Murray, KY, Nhamundá, 1992.
Jeannie Waxenfelter, Russellville, AR, Prainha, 1991.
Cynthia Anne Wells, Beech Street Baptist, Texarkana, AR, Jurutí, 1988.
Connie Wells, Prestonwood Baptist, Dallas, TX, Castanhanduba, 1992, 1993.
Alyssa Welwood, Prestonwood Baptist, Dallas, TX, Castanhanduba, 1992.
Nancy Welwood, Prestonwood Baptist, Dallas, TX, Mamaurú, 1991; Castanhanduba, 1992.
Kelli White, Gracemont Baptist, Tulsa, OK, Estrada Oito, 1989.
Kelly White, Gracemont Baptist, Tulsa, OK, Estrada Oito, 1989.
Tim Whitney, FBC, Russellville, AR, Jurutí, 1993.
Wanda Williams, First and Second Baptist, Arkadelphia, AR, Rio de Janeiro, 1989 (helped install computer system at Brasilian Home Mission Board).
Dana Young, Madisonville, KY, Aveiro, January 27, 1989–January 7, 1990.

Carrie Zerkel, First United Methodist, Joplin, MO, Aveiro, 1994.
Pam Ziegler, FBC, Lakeland, FL, Aveiro, 1992.
Susann Zimmer, Coral Baptist, Coral Springs, FL, Aveiro, 1992.

Construction

Bill Adams, Jr., FBC, Murray, KY, Barrheiras, 1988.
Duane Adams, FBC, Murray, KY, Cuminá, 1994.
Robert Adams, Private Group, McKinney, TX, Aveiro, 1992.
Jerry Alexander, FBC, Russellville, AR, Soure, 1988.
Frank Almaguer, Prestonwood Baptist, Dallas, TX, Castanhanduba, 1993.
Dwight Baber, Palm Lake, FL, Baptist Association, Santa Maria, 1990.
Mike Baber, Palm Lake, FL, Baptist Association Santa Maria, 1990.
Frank Babb, Private Group, Aveiro, 1992.
Jeff Bagby, Gracemont Baptist, Tulsa, OK, Belterra, 1990.
Max Bailey, Murray, Ky, Nhamundá, 1992.
Charles (Chuck) Banken, Gracemont Baptist, Tulsa, OK, Itaituba, 1988.
Larry Barton, FBC, Hope, AR, Tapará, 1986; Aveiro, 1990.
Brian Bateman, AR/FL Group, Cuparí, 1994.
Jeff Bearden, First and Second Baptist, Arkadelphia, AR, Brasilia Legal, 1989.
Dwain Bell, FBC, Murray, KY, Lago Sapacuá, 1991; Cuminá, 1994.
Steve Bilello, Prestonwood Baptist, Dallas, TX, Castanhanduba, 1992.
Mason Billington, FBC, Lakeland, FL, Santa Cruz, 1990.
Bill Binkley, Coral Springs, FL, Group, Aveiro, 1992.
Jeff Blackard, Prestonwood Baptist, Dallas, TX, Mamaurú, 1991; Castanhanduba, 1992; Maicurú, 1993.
Brent Allen Blomquist, Twin Lakes Baptist, Mountain Home, AR, Óbidos, 1994.
Buddy Bolton, Vian Baptist, Vian, OK, Monte Sião, 1989.
Dan Bograjis, FBC, Orlando, FL, Jurutí, 1993.
Cloyd Braswell, Private Group, Aveiro, 1992.
Bob Brian, Palm Lake, FL, Baptist Assn,, Santa Maria, 1990.
Glen Bristow, Beech Street Baptist, Texarkana, AR, Jurutí, 1988.

Jim Bullock, First Southern Baptist, Del City, OK, Aveiro, 1989.
Charlie Burnett, Harmony Heights Baptist, Joplin, MO, Tumbira, 1992; Arapiuns, 1994.
Leonard Burkhart, FBC, Lakeland, FL, Santa Cruz, 1990; Aveiro, 1992.
Alan Burks, Prestonwood Baptist, Dallas, TX, Castanhanduba, 1993.
Lantz Burvant, Coral Baptist, Coral Springs, FL, Santarém (Maracana), 1990.
Rev. Mike Buster, Prestonwood Baptist, Dallas, TX, Mamaurú, 1991.
Jack Caldwell, Gracemont Baptist, Tulsa, OK, Estrada Oito, 1989.
Russ Caldwell, Gracemont Baptist, Tulsa, OK, Itaituba, 1988.
Joshua Cales, Harmony Heights Baptist, Joplin, MO, Arapiuns, 1994.
Cecil Camp, FBC, Lakeland, FL, Santa Cruz, 1990.
Alan Carnahan, FBC, Russellville, AR, Salva Terra, 1988.
Herbert (Grady) Carroll, FBC, Albuquerque, NM, Fordlândia, 1990.
Don (Mr. C) Carter, Private Group, Aveiro, 1992.
Gary Castor, First United Methodist, Joplin, MO, Aveiro, 1994.
Perry Cavitt, FBC, Murray, KY, Barrheiras, 1988; Aveiro, 1989; Lago Sapacuá, 1991; Cuminá, 1994.
Randy Childs, FBC, Russellville, AR, Soure, 1988; Beech Street Baptist, Texarkana, AR, Jurutí, 1988, First and Second Baptist, Arkadelphia, AR, Brasilia Legal, 1989.
Ron (Sonny) Churchill, FBC, Murray, KY, Cuminá, 1994.
Larry Clark, Gracemont Baptist, Tulsa, OK, Estrada Oito, 1989.
Gene Connally, First Southern, Del City, OK, Aveiro, 1989.
Steve Connor, Prestonwood Baptist, Dallas, TX, Mamaurú, 1991; Private Group, Aveiro, 1992.
Jerry Coon, FBC, Orlando, FL, Santarém (Nova República), 1990.
James Crabill, Russellville, AR/Orlando, FL, Cuparí, 1994.
Ken Crain, First and Second Baptist, Arkadelphia, AR, Brasilia Legal, 1989.
Darrell Davis, Gracemont Baptist, Tulsa, OK, Belterra, 1990.
Ron Davis, FBC, Russellville, AR, Soure, 1988; FBC, Murray, KY, Barrheiras, 1988; Palm Lake, FL, Baptist Association, Santa Maria, 1990; FBC, Albuquerque, NM, Fordlândia, 1990.
Walter Decker, Coral Baptist, Coral Springs, FL, Santarém (Maracana), 1990; Aveiro, 1992.
José Delgado, Coral Baptist, Coral Springs, FL, Aveiro, 1992.

Bill Dixon, FBC, Russellville, AR, Soure, 1988; First and Second Baptist, Arkadelphia, AR, Brasilia Legal, 1989.
David Dixon, First and Second Baptist, Arkadelphia, AR, Brasilia Legal, 1989.
Chris Doerge, Calvary Baptist, Joplin, MO, São Luiz, 1991; Harmony Heights Baptist, Joplin, MO, Tumbira, 1992.
Roy Dunagan, First Southern Baptist, Del City, OK, Aveiro, 1989; Terra Santa, 1990.
Mike Dyer, Private Group, Aveiro, 1992.
Gary Edwards, Vian Baptist, Vian, OK, Santa Maria, 1992.
Jeff Elmquist, Russellville, AR/Orlando, FL, Cuparí, 1994.
Ron Elliott, Gracemont Baptist, Tulsa, OK, Estrada Oito, 1989; Aveiro, December 27, 1989–January 7, 1990.
Greg Estep, Harmony Heights Baptist, Joplin, MO, Arapiuns, 1994.
Tom Evans, Southwood Baptist, Tulsa, OK, Flexal, 1993.
Bob Ewing, FBC, Albuquerque, NM, Fordlândia, 1990; Aveiro, 1992.
Marshall Flournoy, FBC, Orlando, FL, Santarém (Nova República), 1990.
Norman Floyd, Coral Baptist, Coral Springs, FL, Santarém (Maracana), 1990.
Randy Foust, First United Methodist, Joplin, MO, Aveiro, 1994.
Fred Frerer, Calvary Baptist, Joplin, MO, São Luiz, 1991.
Herbert S. Gay, Twin Lakes Baptist, Mountain Home, AR, Aveiro, February and April 1994.
Kelly Gienger, Gracemont Baptist, Tulsa, OK, Itaituba, 1988.
Terry Goff, Harmony Heights Baptist, Joplin, MO, Tumbira, 1992; Arapiuns, 1993, 1994.
Bryan Goodman, First Southern, Del City, OK, Aveiro, 1989; Terra Santa, 1990, 1994.
Chris Grabowski, FBC, Albuquerque, NM, Fordlândia, 1990.
Rev. James Greenslade, Twin Lakes Baptist, Mountain Home, AR, Óbidos, 1993, 1994.
Glen Grogan, FBC, Murray KY, Cuminá, 1994.
Dr. Stan Groppel, FBC, Murray, KY, Barrheiras, 1988.
Bill Gruer, Prestonwood Baptist, Dallas, TX, Castanhanduba, 1992.
Larry Gulich, FBC, Russellville, AR, Soure, 1988.
Buddy Hamilton, Vian Baptist, Vian, OK, Monte Sião, 1989.
Mike Hamilton, Gracemont Baptist, Tulsa, OK, Estrada Oito, 1989.

Gary Haralson, First United Methodist, Joplin, MO, Aveiro, 1994.
Darrell Hardman, Twin Lakes Baptist, Mountain Home, AR, Óbidos, 1993, 1994.
Jim Hardman, FBC, Orlando, FL, Jurutí Velho, 1993.
Larry Harrison, FBC, Russellville, AR, Soure, 1988.
Larry Hart, Vian Baptist, Vian, OK, Monte Sião, 1989.
Jim James Hatfield, Prestonwood Baptist, Dallas, TX, Castanhanduba, 1992; Flexal, 1993; Jurutí, 1994.
Allen Haun, Gracemont Baptist, Tulsa, OK, Estrada Oito, 1989.
Richard Henninger, Murray, KY, Aveiro, Dec 27, 1989–January 7, 1990.
Boyd Hickinbotham, Salem, AR, Prainha, 1991.
Archie Hicks, Coral Baptist, Coral Springs, FL, Satarém (Maracana), 1990.
David Hicks, Coral Baptist, Coral Springs, FL, Santarém (Maracana), 1990.
Richard Hicks, Russellville, AR/Orlando, FL, Cuparí, 1994.
Rick Hieb, Private Group, Aveiro, 1992.
Bob Hoebeke, Prestonwood Baptist, Dallas, TX, Mamaurú, 1991.
Matthew Hooyer, Twin Lakes Baptist, Mountain Home, AR, Óbidos, 1993.
Paul Hooyer, Twin Lakes Baptist, Mountain Home, AR, Óbidos, 1993, 1994.
Henry Hubby, Prestonwood Baptist, Dallas, TX, Castanhanduba, 1993.
Kenny Imes, FBC, Murray, KY, Barrheiras, 1988.
Scott Imgrund, Prestonwood Baptist, Dallas, TX, Jurutí, 1994.
Sam Jackson, Private Group, Aveiro, 1992.
Chris Joyner, Private Group, Aveiro, 1992.
Dave Kaltenbach, Prestonwood Baptist, Dallas, TX, Castanhanduba, 1993.
Paul Key, FBC, Murray, KY, Barrheiras, 1988.
Ron Kinney, Private Group, Aveiro, 1992.
Don Knobler, Prestonwood Baptist, Dallas, TX, Castanhanduba, 1993; Jurutí.
Brian Kuehn, Calvary Baptist, Joplin, MO, São Luiz, 1991.
David Lancaster, FBC, Murray, KY, Cuminá, 1994.
Michael Lauden, Vian Baptist, Vian, OK, Monte Sião, 1989.

Stacey Leavell, Russellville, AR, Santa Maria, 1992.
Don Lee, FBC, Murray, KY, Cuminá, 1994.
Richard Lee, Private Group, Aveiro, 1992.
Ken Lisk, Gracemont Baptist, Tulsa, OK, Itaituba, 1988.
Pat Lovelace, Gracemont Baptist, Tulsa, OK, Estrada Oito, 1989; Belterra, 1990.
Dr. Paul Lyons, FBC, Murray, KY, Barrheiras, 1988.
Frank Major, FBC, Murray, KY, Barrheiras, 1988.
Andrew (Pete) Mann, Southwood Baptist, Tulsa, OK, Flexal, 1993.
Kody Mason, First Southern, Del City, OK, Aveiro, 1989; Vian Baptist, Vian, OK, Monte Sião, 1989; First Southern, Del City, OK, Terra Santa, 1990.
Terry Mason, Private Group, Aveiro, 1992.
Mike Mathers, FBC, Lakeland, FL, Santa Cruz, 1990; Aveiro, 1992.
Mark Mayberry, Calvary Baptist, Joplin, MO, São Luiz, 1991.
Bobby McDermitt, Prestonwood Baptist, Dallas, TX, Castanhanduba, 1993.
Kenneth McElveen, Prairie Grove, AR, Aveiro, 1994.
Randall McKelroy, Gracemont Baptist, Tulsa, OK, Itaituba, 1988.
Rich Medlin, FBC, Orlando, FL, Santarém (Nova República), 1990.
Guy Mendrow, Prestonwood Baptist, Dallas, TX, Sapucaía, 1991; Private Group, 1992.
Henry Meeks, Private Group, Aveiro, 1992.
Larry Marchant, Southwood Baptist, Tulsa, OK, Flexal, 1993.
Walter Migdal, FBC, Albuquerque, NM, Aveiro, 1992.
Robert Millar, FBC, Albuquerque, NM, Fordlândia, 1990.
John Miller, Southwood Baptist, Tulsa, OK, Flexal, 1993.
Mike Miller, FBC, Russellville, AR, Soure, 1988; Palm Lake, FL, Baptist Association, Santa Maria, 1990; Prainha, 1991; FBC, Russellville, Jurutí, 1993.
Ramon Miller, Palm Lake, FL, Baptist Association, Santa Maria, 1990.
Tip Miller, FBC, Murray, KY, Barrheiras, 1988; Lago Sapacuá, 1991.
Leonard Monroe, Beech Street Baptist, Texarkana, AR, Jurutí, 1988.
Steve Morrison, Russellville, AR, Prainha, 1991 (see *Witnessing*).
Bill Mulchi, FBC, Orlando, FL, Jurutí Velho, 1993.
Jess Mutz, First United Methodist, Joplin, MO, Aveiro, 1994.
Vernon Nance, FBC, Murray, KY, Barrheiras, 1988; Aveiro, December 27, 1989–January 7, 1990.

Jim Nassar, FBC, Orlando, FL, Jurutí Velho, 1993; Russellville, AR/Orlando, FL, Cuparí, 1994.
Richard Neal, Murray, KY, Aveiro, December 27, 1989–January 7, 1990.
Dan Nichols, FBC, Albuquerque, NM, Fordlândia, 1990.
Mike Nixon, Prestonwood Baptist, Dallas, TX, Castanhanduba, 1992; Maicurú, 1993.
David L. Osmond, First and Second Baptist, Arkadelphia, AR, Brasilia Legal, 1989.
Richard Overmier, FBC, Albuquerque, NM, Fordlândia, 1990; Aveiro, 1992.
Eugene Owen, Palm Lake, FL, Baptist Association, Santa Maria, July 4– 15, 1990; FBC, Albuquerque, NM, Fordlândia, July 18–29, 1990; Gracemont Baptist, Tulsa, OK, Belterra, August 1–12, 1990; Fordlândia, 1991; Aveiro, 1994.
Bob Parks, Gracemont Baptist, Tulsa, OK, Itaituba, 1988; Coral Baptist, Coral Springs, FL, Santarém (Maracana), 1990; Maicurú, 1993; Arapiuns, 1994.
Gary Patton, Gracemont Baptist, Tulsa, OK, Itaituba, 1988.
Wayne Perego, Vian Baptist, Vian, OK, Santa Maria, 1992 (see *Bible School*).
Earl Perry, First United Methodist, Joplin, MO, Aveiro, 1994.
Mark Pharo, Prestonwood Baptist, Dallas, TX, Mamaurú, 1991; Castanhanduba, 1992; Flexal, 1993; Jurutí.
James Pinneo, Gracemont Baptist, Tulsa, OK, Estrada Oito, 1989; Belterra, 1990 (see *Witnessing*).
Bo Pittman, FBC, Orlando, FL, Santarém (Nova República), 1990; Jurutí Velho, 1993; Russellville, AR/Orlando, FL, Cuparí, 1994.
Stephen Polan, FBC, Albuquerque, NM, Fordlândia, 1990 (deceased, 1993).
Jim Ponder, First Southern Baptist, Del City, OK, Aveiro, 1989.
Max Pruegert, First Southern, Del City, OK, Aveiro, 1989; Terra Santa, 1990.
Miles Pruegert, First Southern, Del City, OK, Terra Santa, 1990.
Jim Pruitt, First Baptist, Lakeland, FL, Santa Cruz, 1990.
Buddy Pugh, Coral Baptist, Coral Springs, FL, Aveiro, 1992.
Jerry Purvis, Prestonwood Baptist Church, Dallas, TX, Jurutí, 1994.
Carlo Raimeri, First Baptist, Lakeland, FL, Santa Cruz, 1990.

Ken Ramsey, First and Second Baptist, Arkadelphia, AR, Brasilia Legal, 1989.
Harold Reed, FBC, Russellville, AR, Soure, 1988.
Robert Rea, Prestonwood Baptist, Dallas, TX, Mamaurú, 1991.
Jim Rentner, Coral Baptist, Coral Springs, FL, Santarém (Maracana), 1990.
Ken Rinehart, Gracemont Baptist, Tulsa, OK, Itaituba, 1988; Estrada Oito; Belterra, 1990; Fordlândia, 1991.
Leonard Robertson, Private Group, Aveiro, 1992.
Tom Rocker, First Baptist, Lakeland, FL, Santa Cruz, 1990; Aveiro, 1992.
Randal Rogers, Vian, OK, Nhamundá, 1992.
Ed Rumple, Gracemont Baptist, Tulsa, OK, Fordlândia, 1991.
Allen Russell, FBC, Murray, KY, Lago Sapacuá, 1991.
Roberto Salinas, Private Group, Aveiro, 1992.
John Salisbury, FBC, Lakeland, FL, Aveiro, 1992.
Warren Samuels, Prestonwood Baptist, Dallas, TX, Castanhanduba, 1990.
Quentin Saragusa, Prestonwood Baptist, Dallas, TX, Castanhanduba, 1993.
Truett Scarborough, FBC, Albuquerque, NM, Aveiro, 1992.
Preston Scheurich, Calvary Baptist, Joplin, MO, São Luiz, 1991.
Jed Schlegal, Harmony Heights Baptist, Joplin, MO, Tumbira, 1992.
Mark Schnitzius, Private Group, Aveiro, 1992.
Michael L. Seal, FBC, Russellville, AR, Soure, 1988.
Don Searcy, Private Group, Aveiro, 1992.
Wayne Sebrell, FBC, Albuquerque, NM, Aveiro, 1992.
Noble Seely, Private Group, Aveiro, 1992.
Dennis Sharp, FBC, Murray, KY, Lago Sapacuá, 1991.
George Shilling, FBC, Orlando, FL, Santarém (Nova República), 1990.
Dan Shipley, FBC, Murray, KY, Barrheiras, 1988; Lago Sapacuá, 1991; Cuminá, 1994.
Ken Shipley, FBC, Murray, KY, Lago Sapacuá, 1991.
Leonard Shipley, Private Group, Aveiro, 1992.
Mike Shipman, Private Group, Aveiro, 1992.
Curt Sims, Harmony Heights Baptist, Joplin, MO, Arapiuns, 1993.
Curtis Sims, Harmony Heights Baptist, Joplin, MO, Arapiuns, 1993.

Brian Skellenger, FBC, Orlando, FL, Jurutí Velho, 1993.
Bob Smith, FBC, Orlando, FL, Jurutí Velho, 1993.
Jack Smith, Prestonwood Baptist, Dallas, TX, Mamaurú, 1991.
Ken Smith, FBC, Orlando, FL, Santarém (Nova República), 1990.
Roddy Smith, Palm Lake, FL, Baptist Association, Santa Maria, 1990.
Ken Smith, FBC, Orlando, FL, Santarém (Nova República), 1990.
Roddy Smith, Palm Lake, FL, Baptist Association, Santa Maria, 1990.
Jim Smyth, Prestonwood Baptist, Dallas, TX, Castanhanduba, 1992.
Tom Sokolski, FBC, Lakeland, FL, Santa Cruz, 1990.
Mark Stanford, Gracemont Baptist, Tulsa, OK, Belterra, 1990.
Samuel Stanton, Beech Street Baptist, Texarkana, AR, Jurutí, 1988.
Steve Stauffer, Private Group, Aveiro, 1992.
Gordon Steele, Coral Baptist, Coral Springs, FL, Aveiro, 1992.
Jeff Stewart, FBC, Murray, KY, Cuminá, 1994.
Coy Stone, Viola, AR, Prainha, 1991; Santa Maria, 1992; Maicurú, 1993.
Jerry Stone, Prestonwood Baptist, Dallas, TX, Castanhanduba, 1992.
Tom Straley, Coral Baptist, Coral Springs, FL, Santarém (Maracana), 1990.
Tony Summers, Gracemont Baptist, Tulsa, OK, Itaituba, 1988; Estrada Oito, 1989.
Creston Swaim, FBC, Orlando, FL, Santarém (Nova República), 1990.
Hal Thomas, Prestonwood Baptist, Dallas, TX, Castanhanduba, 1993.
Kevin Thomas, FBC, Murray, KY, Lago Sapacuá, 1991.
Clarence Thompson, First and Second Baptist, Arkadelphia, AR, Brasilia Legal, 1989.
Jed Thompson, Prestonwood Baptist, Dallas, TX, Sapucaía, 1991; Private Group, Aveiro, 1992.
Roy Thompson, Vian Baptist, Vian, OK, Prainha, 1991; Santa Maria, 1992.
Vic Thompson, Gracemont Baptist, Tulsa, OK, Itaituba, 1988.
Mark Tippetts, Twin Lakes Baptist, Mountain Home, AR, Óbidos, 1993.
John Tirone, Palm Lake, FL, Baptist Association, Santa Maria, 1990.
Wes Terrell, FBC, Orlando, FL, Santarém (Nova República), 1990.
David Travis, FBC, Murray, KY, Barrheiras, 1988.

Jerrad Trombley, Harmony Heights Baptist, Joplin, MO, Arapiuns, 1993.
Mark Turner, Smyrna, GA, Aveiro, December 27, 1989–January 7, 1990.
Tip Turner, Prestonwood Baptist Church, Dallas, TX, Jurutí, 1994.
Mike Ussery, FBC, Russellville, AR, Soure, 1988.
Randy Vigneaux, First United Methodist, Joplin, MO, Aveiro, 1994.
Jim Ward, Gracemont Baptist, Tulsa, OK, Belterra, 1990.
Jimmie Washer, Murray, KY, Aveiro, December 27, 1989–January 17, 1990.
Jack Waxenfelter, Palm Lake, FL, Baptist Association, Santa Maria, 1990; Prainha, 1991.
Curt Welwood, Prestonwood Baptist, Dallas, TX, Mamaurú, 1991; FBC, Lakeland, FL, Aveiro, 1992.
Richard (Dick) Westerfield, Coral Baptist, Coral Springs, FL, Santarém (Maracana), 1990.
Rick White, Itaituba, 1988; Aveiro, 1990; Belterra, 1990; Jurutí area, 1991; Jurutí Velho, 1993.
David Williams, Viola, AR, Santa Maria, 1992; Maicurú, 1993.
Don Williams, Beech Street Baptist, Texarkana, AR, Jurutí, 1988.
Bud Wilson, FBC, Albuquerque, NM, Fordlândia, 1990.
Dr. Ken Winters, FBC, Murray, KY, Barrheiras, 1988.
E. J. Wood, FBC, Murray, KY, Lago Sapacuá, 1991; Cuminá, 1994.
Melvin Wright, Beech Street Baptist, Texarkana, AR, Jurutí, 1988.
John Yarusevich, Coral Baptist, Coral Springs, FL, Santarém (Maracana), 1990.
Don Yeager, Gracemont Baptist, Tulsa, OK, Itaituba, 1988.
Chuck Young, FBC, Orlando, FL, Santarém (Nova República), 1990.
David Young, FBC, Murray, KY, Barrheiras, 1988.
Lloyd Zila, FBC, Albuquerque, NM, Fordlândia, 1990; Aveiro, 1992.

Dental

Dr. Charles (Chick) Ainley DDS, Beech Street Baptist, Texarkana, AR, Jurutí, 1988.
Dr. Tim Becker DDS, First Southern, Del City, OK, Aveiro, 1989.

Dr. Thomas Cable DDS, FBC, Albuquerque, NM, Aveiro; Russellville, AR/Orlando, FL, Cuparí, 1994.

Margaret Cales, Calvary Baptist, Joplin, MO, São Luiz, 1991; Harmony Heights Baptist, Joplin, MO, Tumbira, 1992.

Dr. Dwaine Cales DDS, Calvary Baptist, Joplin, MO, São Luiz, 1991; Harmony Heights Baptist, Tumbira, May, 1992; Arapiuns, July 1993; Arapiuns, 1994.

Dr. Ron Cansler, First United Methodist, Joplin, MO, Aveiro, 1994.

Miranda Childs, First and Second Baptist, Arkadelphia, AR, Brasilia Legal, 1989.

Dr. Ricky Davison DDS, FBC, Albuquerque, NM, Fordlândia, 1990; Gracemont Baptist, Tulsa, OK, Fordlândia, 1991.

Dr. Mark Denny DDS, Prestonwood Baptist, Dallas, TX, Mamaurú, 1991, 1993.

Terrie Duvall, Russellville, AR/Orlando, FL, Cuparí, 1994.

Tricia Elliott, Gracemont Baptist, Tulsa, OK, Estrada Oito, 1989; Aveiro, December 27, 1989–January 7, 1990.

Dr. Mike Ellis DDS, Prestonwood Baptist, Dallas, TX, Castanhanduba, 1993.

Tamara Lynn Fain, Twin Lakes Baptist, Mountain Home, AR, Óbidos, 1994.

Sharon Goodrum, FBC, Albuquerque, NM, Fordlândia, 1990.

Cheri Gregory RN, Harmony Heights Baptist, Joplin, MO, Arapiuns, 1994.

Dr. Daniel G. Fields, Oral Surgeon, FBC, Russellville, AR, Soure. 1988.

Betsy Harris, Palm Lake, FL, Baptist Association, Santa Maria, 1990; FBC, Murray, KY, Lago Sapacuá, 1991.

Pat Foster, Gracemont Baptist, Tulsa, OK, Belterra, 1990.

Cindy Goff, Calvary Baptist, Joplin, MO, São Luiz, 1991, Arapiuns, 1994.

Earl Hagar, Twin Lakes Baptist, Mountain Home, AR, Óbidos, 1993, 1994.

Dale Hancock, FBC, Paducah, KY, Oriximiná, 1994.

Dr. Jimmy Hankins DDS, First and Second Baptist, Arkadelphia, AR, Brasilia Legal, 1989.

Linda Hardman, Twin Lakes Baptist, Mountain Home, AR, Brasilia Legal, 1992; Óbidos, 1993.

Diana Hart, First Southern Baptist, Del City, OK, Aveiro, May, 1989; Vian Baptist, Vian, OK, Monte Sião, August, 1989.

Dr. Charles Hartsfield DDS, Gracemont Baptist, Tulsa, OK, Fordlândia, 1991.

Juanita (Nita) Harris, Twin Lakes Baptist, Mountain Home, AR, Óbidos, 1994.

Sandy Hodges, Viola, AR, Prainha, 1991; Santa Maria, 1992; Maicurú, 1993.

Dr. Johnny Hollier DDS, Palm Lake FL, Baptist Association, Santa Maria, July 1990; First Southern, Del City, OK, Terra Santa, August 1990; Prainha, 1991; Brasilia Legal, 1992.

Dr. Fred Kapple DDS, Gracemont Baptist, Tulsa, OK, Itaituba, 1988.

Sonja King, FBC, Albuquerque, NM, Aveiro, 1992; Russellville, AR/Orlando, FL, Cuparí, 1994.

Mary Kirkland, Gracemont Baptist, Tulsa, OK, Estrada Oito, 1989.

Karen Loy RDH, Oklahoma City, OK, Terra Santa, 1994.

Rosie McPeak, Lantana, FL, Santa Maria, 1992 (see also *Bible School*).

Dr. Clint Miner DDS, Vian Baptist, Vian, OK, Monte Sião, 1989.

Debra Montgomery, Prestonwood Baptist, Dallas, TX, Mamaurú, 1991.

Dr. Jeff Montgomery DDS, Prestonwood Baptist, Mamaurú, 1991.

Stephen Osmon, First and Second Baptist, Arkadelphia, AR, Brasilia Legal, 1989.

Dr. J. D. Outland DDS, FBC, Lakeland, FL, Santa Cruz, 1990; FBC, Murray, KY, Lago Sapacuá, 1991.

Dr. Alan Owen DDS, First Southern, Del City, OK, Aveiro, 1989.

Dr. Jeff Parker, Gracemont Baptist, Tulsa, OK, Belterra, 1990.

Alice Perry, Harmony Heights Baptist, Joplin, MO, Arapiuns, 1994.

James Phelan, FBC, Albuquerque, NM, Aveiro, 1992.

Barbara Plankenhorn, FBC, Lakeland, FL, Santa Cruz, 1990.

Dr. Joe Rexroat DDS, FBC, Murray, KY, Barrheiras, 1988.

Dr. Don Roberts DDS, Oklahoma City, OK, Terra Santa, 1994.

Robbie Rudolph, FBC, Murray, KY, Barrheiras, 1988.

Dr. Tim Shannon DDS, Prestonwood Baptist, Dallas, TX, Jurutí, 1994.

Dr. Randall (Randy) Simpson DDS, Twin Lakes Baptist, Mountain Home, AR, Óbidos, 1994.

Dr. Kinney Slaughter DDS, FBC, Paducah, KY, Oriximiná, 1994.

Dr. Mickey Sehova DDS, Oklahoma City, OK, Terra Santa, 1994.

Dr. Charles (Buzz) Stetler DDS, Prestonwood Baptist, Dallas, TX, Castanhanduba, 1992.
Joyce Thompson, Vian Baptist, Vian, OK, Monte Sião, 1989; Prainha, 1991; Maicurú, 1993.
Virginia Holt Turner, Gracemont Baptist, Tulsa, OK, Itaituba, 1988; Belterra, 1990; Calvary Baptist, Joplin, MO, São Luiz, 1991.
Dr. Jay Wells DDS, FBC, Murray, KY, Cuminá, 1994.
Jennifer White, Southwood Baptist, Tulsa, OK, Flexal, 1993.
Dr. Kelvin White MD, Murray, KY, Mamundá, 1992.
Jane Williams, Prestonwood Baptist, Dallas, TX, Mamaurú, 1991; Castanhanduba, 1992.
Dr. Bruce Williams DDS, Gracemont Baptist, Tulsa, OK, Belterra, 1990.
Dr. Jim Williams DDS, First United Methodist, Joplin, MO, Aveiro, 1994.
Dr. Alan Winberry DDS, Gracemont Baptist, Tulsa, OK, Estrada Oito, 1989; Aveiro, December 27, 1989–January 7, 1990; Jurutí, 1991; Santa Maria, 1992 (see also *Witnessing*).
Linda Winberry, Gracemont Baptist, Tulsa, OK, Estrada Oito, 1989; Aveiro, December 27, 1989–January 17, 1990.
Gina Shipley Winchester, FBC, Murray, KY, Barrheiras, 1988.
David Winnett, Harmony Heights Baptist. Joplin, MO, Arapiuns, 1993.
Lou Wright, Vian Baptist, Vian, OK, Monte Sião, 1989.

Medical

Dr. David Alkek MD, Prestonwood Baptist, Dallas, TX, Castanhanduba, 1992, 1993.
Sharon Jane Antwine RN, Twin Lakes Baptist, Mountain Home, AR, Óbidos, 1994.
Dr. Clegg Austin MD, FBC, Murray, KY, Lago Sapacuá, 1991; Cuminá, 1994.
Faye Austin RN, FBC, Murray, KY, Lago Sapacuá, 1991; Cuminá, 1994.
John Michael Austin, FBC, Murray, KY, Lago Sapacuá, 1991.
Earnie Baldridge PA, FBC, Albuquerque, NM, Fordlândia, 1990;

Gracemont Baptist, Tulsa, OK, Fordlândia, 1991; FBC, Albuquerque, NM, Aveiro, 1992.
Dr. Ray Bandy MD, Gracemont Baptist, Tulsa, OK, Belterra, 1990.
Brenda Biles, Southwood Baptist, Tulsa, OK, Flexal, 1993.
Bob Bobbitt, Cincinnati, Ohio, Maicurú, 1993.
Teresa Bovee RN, Moore, OK, Brasilia Legal, 1992; Terra Santa, 1994.
Dr. Stanley Bradley MD, FBC, Russellville, AR, Soure, 1988; Nhamundá, 1993; Cuparí, 1994.
Barbara Bremer RN, Twin Lakes Baptist, Mountain Home, AR, Óbidos, 1994.
Kristal Briley RN, Prestonwood Baptist, Dallas, TX, Jurutí, 1994.
Becky Buege LPN, Harmony Heights Baptist, Joplin, MO, Tumbira, 1992.
Amy Brumfield, Harmony Heights Baptist, Joplin, MO, Arapiuns, 1994.
Oleta Burkeen RN, FBC, Murray, KY, Lago Sapacuá, 1991.
Dr. James Carter MD, FBC, Russellville, AR, Soure, 1988; Palm Lake, FL, Baptist Association, Santa Maria, 1990; Prainha, 1991.
Jamie Carter, FBC, Russellville, AR, Soure, 1988.
Donna Cheatham RN, Russellville, AR/Orlando, FL, Cuparí, 1994.
Naomi Cherry RN, Russellville, AR/Orlando, FL, Cuparí, 1994.
Tina Chronister, Palm Lake, FL, Baptist Association, Santa Maria, 1990; Nhamundá, 1992 (see also *Optometry*).
Linda Clark RN, FBC, Murray, KY, Cuminá, 1994.
Jana Cable RN, Joplin, MO, Jurutí, 1991.
Cherry Conatser RN, Prestonwood Baptist, Dallas, TX, Mamaurú, 1991.
Pam Cochran, Oklahoma City, OK, Terra Santa, 1994.
Susan Cooper, FBC, Paducah, KY, Oriximiná, 1994.
Dr. John Cox DO, Calvary Baptist, Joplin, MO, São Luiz, 1991; First United Methodist, Joplin, MO, Aveiro, 1994.
Justin Cox, First United Methodist, Joplin, MO, Aveiro, 1994.
Pat Daniels LPN, Oklahoma City, OK, Terra Santa, 1994.
Dr. Richard Crouch MD, FBC, Murray, KY, Barrheiras, 1988.
Karen Davenport RN, Prestonwood Baptist, Dallas, TX, Jurutí, 1994.
Carolyn Davidson RN, Prestonwood Baptist, Dallas, TX, Castanhanduba, 1992.

Dr. Jim Davidson MD, Prestonwood Baptist, Dallas, TX, Mamaurú, 1991; Castanhanduba, 1992; Jurutí, 1994.
Betty Davis RN, First Southern, Del City, OK, Terra Santa, 1990.
Dr. Jerry DeVane MD, FBC, Lakeland, FL, Santa Cruz, 1990; Gracemont Baptist, Tulsa, OK, Fordlândia, 1991.
Dr. Jo Lee DeVane MD, FBC, Lakeland, FL, Santa Cruz, 1990; Gracemont Baptist, Tulsa, OK, Fordlândia, 1991.
Dr. Tim Drehmer MD, First Southern, Del City, OK, Aveiro, 1989.
Dr. Jerry Edwards MD, FBC, Murray, KY, Cuminá, 1994.
Blanche Enriquez RN, Prestonwood Baptist, Dallas, TX, Jurutí, 1994.
Bonnie Evans, Russellville, AR/Orlando, FL, Cuparí, 1994.
Danise Faulk RN, Prestonwood Baptist, Dallas, TX, Jurutí, 1994.
Jan Finn RN, First United Methodist, Joplin, MO, Aveiro, 1994.
Bill Fiaccone RN, Oklahoma City, OK, Terra Santa, 1994.
Ashley Fleniken, Russellville, AR, Santa Maria, 1992.
Nancy Renee Fletcher, Twin Lakes Baptist, Mountain Home, AR, Óbidos, 1994.
Tammy Flowers RN, First Southern, Del City, OK, Aveiro, 1989.
Diane Frie RN, Southwood Baptist, Tulsa, OK, Flexal, 1993.
Mark Giles RN, AR/OK/KY, Nhamundá, 1992.
Sandra Giroldo RN, Prestonwood Baptist, Dallas, TX, Jurutí, 1994.
Dr. Edward Glinski DD, Oklahoma City, OK, Brasilia Legal, 1992; Terra Santa, 1994.
Laura Glinski, Oklahoma City, OK, Terra Santa, 1994.
Judy Greenslade RN, Twin Lakes Baptist, Mountain Home, AR, Óbidos, 1993.
Johnna Hall RN, FBC, Lakeland, FL, Santa Cruz, 1990; Aveiro, 1992.
Ann Harris Armstrong-Haren RN, Calvary Baptist, Joplin, MO, São Luiz, 1991 (deceased, 1993).
Brite Harmon, FBC, Orlando, FL, Jurutí Velho, 1993; Russellville, AR/Orlando, FL, Cuparí, 1994.
Joanie Harris, FBC, Paducah, KY, Oriximiná, 1994.
Dr. Al Harvey DO, First Southern, Del City, OK, Aveiro, May 1989; December 27, 1989–January 7, 1990; Terra Santa, August 1990; Brasilia Legal, 1992; Terra Santa, 1994.
Harvey Heather, First Southern, Del City, OK, Terra Santa, 1990, 1994.
Holly Harvey, First Southern, Del City, OK, Aveiro, December 27, 1989–January 7, 1990; Terra Santa, 1994.

Marsha Harvey, First Southern, Del City, OK, Terra Santa, 1994.
Judy Henninger RN, FBC, Murray, KY, Lago Sapacuá, 1991.
Sharon Hendricks RN. Harmony Heights Baptist, Joplin, MO, Arapiuns, 1994.
Mary Francis Henson, Prestonwood Baptist, Dallas, TX, Castanhanduba, 1993.
Melissa Hicks RN, FBC, Orlando, FL, Jurutí Velho, 1993.
Corine Hiser RN, Twin Lakes Baptist, Mountain Home, AR, Óbidos, 1994.
Rev. John Hodges, Viola, AR, Prainha, 1991; Santa Maria, 1992; Maicurú, 1993.
Joan Hoffman RN, First United Methodist, Joplin, MO, Aveiro, 1994.
Lauren Hollingsworth, FBC, Albuquerque, NM, Fordlândia, 1990.
Diane Holman RN, FBC, Paducah, KY, Orixíminá, 1994.
Velma Hottes, Twin Lakes Baptist, Mountain Home, AR, Óbidos, 1993.
Dr. Lloyd Housman MD, FBC, Paducah, KY, Orixíminá, 1994.
Dr. Russ Howard MD, FBC, Murray, KY, Lago Sapacuá, 1991.
Donna Hubbell RN, FBC, Lakeland, FL, Santa Cruz, 1990.
Juanita Hunt RN, Russellville, AR, Prainha, 1991.
Jenny James Garza RN, Beech Street Baptist, Texarkana, AR, Jurutí, 1988.
Elaine Johnson RN, Calvary Baptist, Joplin, MO, São Luiz, 1991; Harmony Heights Baptist, Joplin, MO, Tumbira, 1992; Arapiuns, 1993.
Dr. William Johnson MD, Gracemont Baptist, Tulsa, OK, Fordlândia, 1991.
Dr. Len Kemp MD, Beech Street Baptist, Texarkana, AR, Jurutí, 1988.
Matt Kimberling, Medical Student, Twin Lakes Baptist, Mountain Home, AR, Óbidos, 1994.
Christine King RN, Harmony Heights Baptist, Joplin, MO, Arapiuns, 1994.
Dr. Gregory Kirk MD, Vian, OK, Maicurú, 1993.
Renee St. Laurent RN, Prestonwood Baptist, Dallas, TX, Jurutí, 1994.
Dr. Damaris Wright Knobler MD, Prestonwood Baptist, Dallas, TX. Castanhanduba, 1993; Jurutí, 1994.
Marie Kohlenberger RN, FBC, Paducah, KY, Orixíminá. 1994.
Dr. Jimmy Laferney MD, FBC, Lakeland, FL, Aveiro, 1992.

Lair Jacquetta LPN, First Southern, Del City, OK, Terra Santa, 1990.
Patti Lester RN, Southwood Baptist, Tulsa, OK, Flexal, 1993.
Dr. Lance Lincoln MD, Twin Lakes Baptist, Mountain Home, AR, Óbidos, 1993, 1994.
Marsha Lisk RN, Gracemont Baptist, Tulsa, OK, Itaituba, 1988.
Sue Loveless RN, Gracemont Baptist, Tulsa, OK, Belterra, 1990.
Mike Lowe, Medical Student, Twin Lakes Baptist, Mountain Home, AR, Óbidos, 1994.
Jeff Luetschwager RN, First United Methodist, Joplin, MO, Aveiro, 1994.
Bill Lyscio, Harmony Heights Baptist, Joplin, MO, Arapiuns, 1993, 1994.
Marsha Mallow, Southwood Baptist, Tulsa, OK, Flexal, 1993.
Ann Mansfield RN, FBC, Paducah, KY, Oriximiná.
Dr. Carl Marquess MD, FBC, Paducah, KY, Oriximiná, 1994.
Dr. Doug Marx MD, Twin Lakes Baptist, Mountain Home, AR, Óbidos, 1993, 1994.
Kevin McCullough EMT, Oklahoma City, OK, Terra Santa, 1994.
Margaret McDonald RN, First United Methodist, Joplin, MO, Aveiro, 1994.
Dr. Brad McElroy MD, FBC, Paducah, KY, Oriximiná, 1994.
Deana McReynolds, FBC, Murray, KY, Cuminá, 1994.
Jeff Mason EMT, Harmony Heights Baptist, Joplin, MO, Arapiuns, 1994.
Susan Monaghan RN, Joplin, MO, Jurutí, 1991.
Betty Morgan RN, FBC, Lakeland, FL, Aveiro, 1992.
Lorrain Morrison RN, Prestonwood Baptist, Dallas, TX, Castanhanduba, 1992, 1993.
Patty Mulchi RN, FBC, Orlando, FL, Jurutí Velho, 1993.
Dr. David Murphy MD, Russellville, AR/Orlando, FL, Cuparí, 1994.
Dr. Ken New MD, Russellville, AR, Nhamundá, 1992.
Chris Newby RN, Joplin, MO, Jurutí area, 1991.
Maureen O'Connell RN, Joplin, MO, Jurutí area, 1991.
Lori Page RN, First Southern Baptist, Del City, OK, Aveiro, 1989; Terra Santa, 1990.
Louise Parsons RN-Anesthesiologist, Vian Baptist, Vian, OK, Monte Sião, 1989 (Deceased, 1992).
Doug Peeler, FBC, Orlando, FL, Jurutí Velho, 1993.

Kevin Penwell, Medical Student, Oklahoma City, OK, Brasilia Legal, 1992; Terra Santa, 1994.

Dr. Milam Pharo MD, Prestonwood Baptist, Dallas, TX, Castanhanduba, 1992; Flexal, 1993; Jurutí, 1994.

Lisa Fitzgerald Pinneo RN, Gracemont Baptist, Tulsa, OK, Itaituba, 1988; Estrada Oito, 1989; Belterra, 1990; Southwood Baptist, Tulsa, OK, Flexal, 1993.

Lin Pinter RN, FBC, Orlando, FL, Jurutí Velho, 1993.

Kay Plumlee RN, Ash Flat, AR, Prainha, 1991; Santa Maria, 1992.

Robin Porter RN, Twin Lakes Baptist, Mountain Home, AR, Óbidos, 1993.

Jo Pottenger RN, First United Methodist, Joplin, MO, Aveiro, 1994.

Dr. Ken Pottenger MD, First United Methodist, Joplin, MO, Aveiro, 1994.

Bonnie Raineri, FBC, Lakeland, FL, Santa Cruz, 1990.

Diane Randolph RN, Prestonwood Baptist, Dallas, TX, Castanhanduba, 1992.

Lori Rhodes, FBC, Murray, KY, Cuminá, 1994.

Ann Rinehart RN, Gracemont Baptist, Tulsa, OK, Itaituba, 1988; Estrada Oito, 1989; Belterra, 1990; Fordlândia, 1991.

Jessie Rinks RN, FBC, Albuquerque, NM, Fordlândia, 1990; Aveiro, 1992.

Dr. Rick Scacewater MD, Harmony Heights Baptist, Joplin, MO, Tumbira, 1992.

Holly Schalchlin, Prestonwood Baptist, Dallas, TX, Mamaurú, 1991.

Dr. Claire Dean Schill, chiropractor, FBC, Orlando, FL, Jurutí Velho, 1993.

Dr. David Shuler DO, Gracemont Baptist, Tulsa, OK, Belterra, 1990; Jurutí area, 1991.

Anne Smith RN, Oklahoma City, OK, Terra Santa, 1994.

Elaine Smith RN, Palm Lake, FL, Baptist Association, Santa Maria, 1990.

Donna Smith, Twin Lakes Baptist, Mountain Home, AR, Óbidos, 1993.

Joan Smith RN, Gracemont Baptist, Tulsa, OK, Belterra, 1990; Fordlândia, 1991.

Keturah Smith, First Southern, Del City, OK, Terra Santa, 1990.

Shari Smith, Medical Student, Harmony Heights Baptist, Joplin, MO, Tumbira, 1992; Arapiuns, 1993.
Barbara Smotherman, FBC, Murray, KY, Barrheiras, 1988.
Tasha Somers, FBC, Paducah, KY, Orixíminá, 1994.
Cheryl Ann Spore RN, Twin Lakes Baptist, Mountain Home, AR, Óbidos, 1993, 1994.
Dr. John Spore MD, Twin Lakes Baptist, Mountain Home, AR, Óbidos, 1993, 1994.
Dr. Pat Sullivan DO, Vian Baptist, Vian, OK, Monte Sião, 1989.
Catherine Swaims RN, FBC, Albuquerque, NM, Fordlândia, 1990.
Mrs. Buddy (Malinda) Teehee RN, Claremore, OK, Monte Sião, 1989.
Clyde Tempel, Anesthsiologist, First and Second Baptist, Arkadelphia, AR, Brasilia Legal, 1989; Calvary Baptist, Joplin, MO, São Luiz, 1991.
Mary Tempel RN, First and Second Baptist, Arkadelphia, AR, Brasilia Legal, 1989.
Renee Thompson RN, Vian Baptist, Vian, OK, Monte Sião, 1989; Jurutí area, 1993.
Dr. Yoland Condrey-Tinkle MD, Twin Lakes Baptist, Mountain Home, AR., Óbidos, 1994.
Rhonda Traue LPN, First Southern, Del City, OK, Aveiro, 1989.
Kathy Turner, Prestonwood Baptist, Dallas, TX, Jurutí, 1994.
Dr. Ken Turner DO, Harmony Heights Baptist, Joplin, MO, Itaituba, 1988; Belterra 1990; São Luiz, 1991; Tumbira, 1992; Arapiuns, 1994.
Lori Webb, Hazel, KY, Brasilia Legal, 1992; Castanhanduba, 1992.
Jessica Well RN, FBC, Russellville, AR, Jurutí, 1993.
Tara Weigand-Hammons RN, First United Methodist, Joplin, MO, Aveiro, 1994.
Rebecca Whitney, Anesthsiologist, FBC, Russellville, AR, Jurutí, 1993.
Nora Williams, Prestonwood Baptist, Dallas, TX, Castanhanduba, 1992.
Beth Wilson, Russellville, AR/Orlando, FL, Cuparí, 1994.
Winnie Wolfe RN, Mammoth Springs, AR, Santa Maria, 1992.
Emeline Sue Wright RN, FBC, Orlando, FL, Jurutí Velho, Cuparí, 1993, 1994.
Dr. Mark Yelderman MD, FBC, Lakeland, FL, Aveiro, 1992.

Lynne York, FBC, Murray, KY, Cuminá, 1994.

Optometry

Jan Baldridge, FBC, Albuquerque, NM, Aveiro, 1992 (see *Bible School*).
Debbie Bost, Salem, AR, Prainha, 1991; Santa Maria, 1992.
Doris Brower, Lantana, FL, Santa Maria, 1992.
Jim Cook, Coral Baptist, Coral Springs, FL, Aveiro, 1992.
Dr. James Courtney OD, FBC, Murray, KY, Barrheiras, 1988.
Tina Chronister, FBC, Russellville, AR, 1993 (see *Medical*).
Claudette Davison, FBC, Albuquerque, NM, Fordlândia, 1990; Gracemont Baptist, Tulsa, OK, Fordlândia, 1991.
Theresa Fannin, FBC, Lakeland, FL, Santa Cruz, 1990.
Frank Fitzgerald, Vian Baptist, Vian, OK, Monte Sião, 1989.
Tim Greer, FBC, Murray, KY, Cuminá, 1994.
Thelma Jean Hill, Twin Lakes Baptist, Mountain Home, AR, Óbidos, 1993, 1994.
Gary Johánson, Russellville, AR/Orlando, FL, Cuparí, 1994.
John Johnson, Palm Lake, FL, Baptist Association, Santa Maria, 1990.
Sandy Johnson, Palm Lake, FL, Baptist Association, Santa Maria, 1990.
Jeanne Perry-Jones, First United Methodist, Joplin, MO, Aveiro, 1994.
Thomas V. Jones, First United Methodist, Joplin, MO, Aveiro, 1994.
Janice Lane, First Southern, Del City, OK, Terra Santa, 1990.
Dr. Spencer Meckstroth OD, First Southern, Del City, OK, Aveiro, 1989; Palm Lake, FL, Baptist Association, Santa Maria; Prestonwood Baptist, Dallas, TX, Mamaurú, 1991.
Dr. Mike Moorehead OD, Prestonwood Baptist, Dallas, TX, Jurutí, 1994.
Rodney Robertson, Prestonwood Baptist, Dallas, TX, Castanhanduba, 1993.
Dr. H. Keith Scott OD, FBC, Russellville, AR, Soure, 1988.
Don Short, Harmony Heights Baptist, Joplin, MO, Tumbira, 1992; Arapiuns, 1993, 1994.
Sue Short, Harmony Heights Baptist, Joplin, MO, Tumbira, 1992; Arapiuns, 1993, 1994.

Dr. John Strakal OD, FBC, Paducah, KY, Oriximiná, 1994.
Dr. Claude Sumerlin PHD, First and Second Baptist, Arkadelphia, AR, Brasilia Legal, 1989.
Helen Thompson, First and Second Baptist churches, Brasilia Legal, 1989.
Janet Thurber, AR/FL Group, Cuparí, 1994.
Judy Young, Greenacres, FL, Santa Maria, l992.
Kurt Wachtendorf, Southwood Baptist, Tulsa, OK, Flexal, 1993.
Patty Wachtendorf, Southwood Baptist, Tulsa, OK, Flexal, 1993.

Pharmacy

Bobetta Baker, Calvary Baptist, Joplin, MO, São Luiz, 1992.
David Scott Baker, Salem, AR, Santa Maria, 1992.
J. T. Baker, Gracemont Baptist, Tulsa, OK, Fordlándia, 1991.
Dr. Scott Baker RPH, Gracemont Baptist, Tulsa, OK, Fordlândia, 1991; Santa Maria, 1992.
Dr. Shields Baker RPH, Harmony Heights Baptist, Joplin, MO, Arapiuns, 1994.
Dr. David L. Barnes RPH, Gracemont Baptist, Tulsa, OK, Itaituba, 1988; Estrada Oito, 1989; Belterra, 1990.
Joe Bradley, Russellville, AR/Orlando, FL, Cuparí, 1994.
Lori Byrnes, Twin Lakes Baptist, Mountain Home, AR, Óbidos, 1993.
Dr. Mark Chronister RPH, FBC, Russellville, AR, Nhamundá, 1992; Jurutí, 1993.
Dr. Harold Cox RPH, Harmony Heights Baptist, Joplin, MO, Tumbira, 1992; Arapiuns, 1993.
Dr. Gary Denton RPH, FBC, Russellville, AR, Jurutí, 1993.
Wayne Elgin, First United Methodist, Joplin, MO, Aveiro, 1994.
Tami Jones, First United Methodist, Joplin, MO, Aveiro, 1994.
Ellen Lyons, Russellville, AR, Brasilia Legal, 1992.
Dr. Randy Morris RPH, Twin Lakes Baptist, Mountain Home, AR, Óbidos, 1993, 1994.
Kathryn Phelan, Phar. Tech., FBC, Albuquerque, NM, Aveiro, 1992.
Judie Riggen, Harmony Heights Baptist, Joplin, MO, Tumbira, 1992; Arapiuns, 1993, 1994.

Martia Schultz, Prestonwood Baptist, Dallas, TX, Sapucaía, 1991.
Laura Lee Shorts, Prestonwood Baptist, Dallas, TX, Castanhanduba, 1992.
Beth Wilson, AR/FL Group, Cuparí, 1994.

Witnessing

Travis Arterbury, Russellville, AR, Soure, 1988.
Rev. Sam Bailey, Twin Lakes Baptist, Mountain Home, AR, Óbidos, 1993.
David Bauman, FBC, Russellville, AR, Jurutí, 1993.
Rev. Wilson Beardsley, Oklahoma City, OK, Terra Santa, 1994.
Don Bentley, Russellville, AR, Brasilia Legal, 1992.
Dennie Bost, Salem, AR, Jurutí, 1991.
Col. John Brink, Viola, AR, Jurutí, 1991.
Rev. Mark Brooks, FBC, Russellville, AR, Soure, 1988.
Rev. John Mark Caton, Prestonwood Baptist, Dallas, TX, 1994.
Dan Caldwell, Vian Baptist, Vian, OK, Monte Sião, 1989.
Cal Chappell, First Southern Baptist, Del City, OK, Aveiro, 1989.
Jim Coley, First Southern, Del City, OK, Aveiro, 1989; Terra Santa, 1990.
Dr. Hershel Cresman, Coral Baptist, Coral Springs, FL, Santarém (Maracana), 1990.
Dr. Stephen P. Davis, FBC, Russellville, AR, Soure, 1988.
Dr. Greg Earwood, FBC, Murray, KY, Barrheiras, 1988.
Mike Forehand, Gracemont Baptist, Tulsa, OK, Itaituba, 1988.
Dr. Rick Frie, Southwood Baptist, Tulsa, OK, Flexal, 1993.
Pat Guinn, First Southern, Del City, OK, Terra Santa, 1990.
Greg Hailey, Calvary Baptist, Joplin, MO, São Luiz, 1991.
Dr. Mike Hailey, FBC, Lakeland, FL, Santa Cruz, 1990.
Sandy Hailey, FBC, Lakeland, FL, Santa Cruz, 1990.
Rev. Joe Haskett, Toccoa, GA, Aveiro, December 27, 1989–January 7, 1990.
Rev. Jim Hawkins, FBC, Paducah, KY, Oriximiná, 1994.
Rev. Welby Jones, Gracemont Baptist, Tulsa, OK, Estrada Oito, 1989; Belterra, 1990.

Barry Limbard, FBC, Russellville, AR, Soure, 1988 (see also *Construction*).
Vickie Limbard, FBC, Russellville, AR, Prainha, 1991.
Jeannie Lyons, FBC, Russellville, AR, Soure, 1988; Prainha, 1991; Brasilia Legal, 1991.
Rev. Jim Maddox, Coral Springs Baptist, Coral Springs, FL, Aveiro, 1992.
Rev. Henry Nager, FBC, Russellville, AR, Soure, 1988.
Dr. Kevin McCallon, FBC, Paducah, KY, Oriximiná, 1994.
Dr. Joe McKinney, Gracemont Baptist, Tulsa, OK, Itaituba, 1988; FBC, Albuquerque, NM, Fordlândia, 1990.
Leonard Monroe, Beech Street Baptist, Texarkana, AR, Jurutí, 1988.
Steve Morrison, Russellville, AR, Prainha, 1991; Brasilia Legal, 1992.
Rev. Boyd Pelley, FBC, Albuquerque, NM, Aveiro, 1992.
James Pinneo, Southwood Baptist, Tulsa, OK, Flexal, 1992 (see also *Construction*).
Ken Pittman, First Southern Baptist, Del City, OK, Aveiro, 1989.
Rev. Randy Shaddox, Gracemont Baptist, Tulsa, OK, Itaituba, 1988.
Rev. James Simmons, FBC, Lakeland, FL, Santa Cruz, 1990.
Paul Snyder, Harmony Heights Baptist, Joplin, MO, Arapiuns, 1993.
Rev. Lewis Spears, Gracemont Baptist, Tulsa, OK, Itaituba, 1988.
Dr. Tim Summers, Harmony Heights Baptist, Joplin, MO, Arapiuns, 1993, 1994.
Rev. Gary Underwood, Beech Street Baptist, Texarkana, AR, Jurutí, 1988.
Dr. Bob Utley, Marshall, TX, Brasilia Legal, 1992.
Lee Walker, First Southern, Del City, OK, Aveiro, 1989.
Brian Winters, Marshall, TX, Brasilia Legal, 1992.
Dr. John Wood, Waco, TX, teacher for Laymen's Institute, 1992, 1993.
Jim Young, Harmony Heights Baptist, Joplin, MO, Arapiuns, 1994.

Miscellaneous

Ronnie Davis, FBC, Russellville, AR, Soure, July, 1988; FBC, Murray, KY, Barreiras, July, 1988 (Bible School).
Ben DeVane, age 9, FBC, Lakeland, FL, Santa Cruz, 1990; Gracemont

Baptist, Tulsa, OK, Fordlândia, 1991 (accompanied physician parents).
Johnson Ellis, Prestonwood Baptist, Dallas, TX, Mamaurú, 1991 (interpreter).
Dr. J. T. Houk, FBC, Albuquerque, NM, Fordlândia, 1990 (fund raiser).
Marion Hughes, Gracemont Baptist, Tulsa, OK, Itaituba, 1988 (photographer).
Kyle Laferney, FBC, Lakeland, FL, Aveiro, 1992 (a minor).
Shaun LePage, Calvary Baptist, Joplin, MO, São Luiz, 1991 (video/evangelism).
Danny Lyons, FBC, Russellville, AR, Soure, 1988; Brasilia Legal, 1992 (physical therapist).
Elsie Monroe, Beech Street Baptist, Texarkana, AR, Jurutí, 1988 (cook).
Bill Reese, FBC, Paducah, KY, Oriximiná, 1994 (photographer).
Rett Scudder, Prestonwood Baptist, Dallas, TX, Mamaurú, 1991 (video).
Dixie Thackston, FBC, Russellville, AR. Brasilia Legal, 1992; Jurutí, 1993 (interpreter).
Adam Welwood, FBC, Lakeland, FL, Aveiro, 1992 (a minor).
Judy White, Aveiro, 1990; Nhamundá. 1992; Jurutí Velho, 1993 (interpreter).

About the Author

Claude Sumerlin lives with his wife of forty-eight years, Katherine, in Arkadelphia, Arkansas. He has retired as professor and chairman of Journalism at Henderson State University in Arkadelphia, while she has retired as periodicals librarian of Ouachita Baptist University, also in Arkadelphia. Both are native Texans.

Claude previously served as head of the Journalism Department and News Bureau at Ouachita and taught journalism and English for ten years in Texas high schools. During summers, he worked at various positions on Tyler, Texas, dailies, including wire editor in 1961 and 1972. He worked sixteen months as a sports writer and assistant sports editor for San Antonio, Texas, dailies.

Sumerlin was graduated as valedictorian of Kingsville, Texas, Henrietta M. King High School, received a B.A. in English/Journalism from Texas A&I, an M.A. in English from Baylor University, and a Ph.D. in Journalism from the University of Missouri. He has received the Dow Newspaper Scholarship and Award for Meritorious Service to Journalism and the Edith Fox King Award of Distinguished Merit from the University of Texas.

He is listed in various regional and national biographies and in five international biographies. He has had articles published regionally, nationally, and internationally, but this is his first long work except his microfilmed doctoral dissertation. The couple has one son, Dr. Neal Sumerlin, chairman of the Chemistry Department at Lynchburg (Virginia) College. Neal and wife Jane have two children.